Mi linda
Mariuta

Este libro va con
todo el amor de tu abuelo
Hugo y lo llevan Ana Ximena
del Rosario y su mami Lela en este su
primer viaje a Arkansas L.R.
Confío te guste mucho que pasen lindas
con sus queridas huéspedes unos
y felices vacaciones de verano
Besos y bendiciones
del abuelo Hugo
Hugo

Nota: Primer viaje para Ana Ximena del Rosario
visitando a sus primitos a Mariita Linda y Alex
gracias por todo su amor para Ximena y Lela

Guatemala, C.A. Arkansas L.R. 13 agosto-84

THE FAMILY LIBRARY OF
HORSES

ENGMA ?

THE FAMILY LIBRARY OF
HORSES

Elwyn Hartley Edwards

OCTOPUS

First published in 1981
by Octopus Books Limited
59 Grosvenor St
London W1

© 1980 Octopus Books Limited

ISBN 0 7064 1458 6

Produced for Octopus by
Theorem Publishing Limited
71–73 Great Portland Street
London W1N 5DH

Printed in Hong Kong

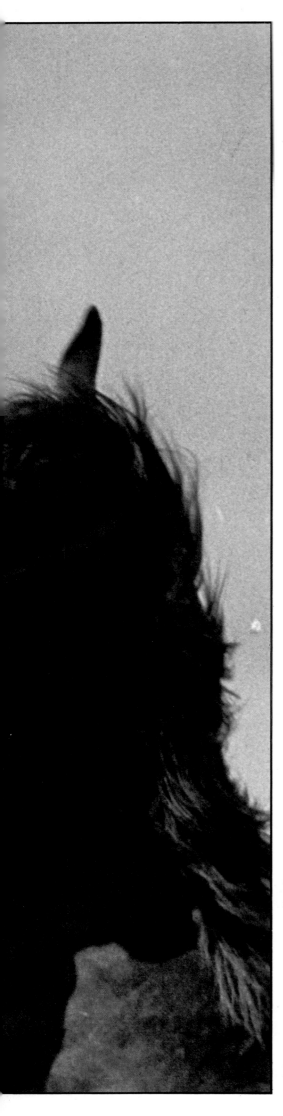

Introduction

More and more people are getting interested in horses—whether they are actually going out and riding them or simply watching a big showjumping spectacular on television. And it is not surprising because the horse world has so much to offer. You do not have to be an experienced rider to enjoy a trekking holiday through glorious mountain scenery. You do not have to compete in a three-day-event to enjoy the thrills and spills, or admire the courage of horses and riders. But it helps to have a basic knowledge of the sport of your choice. This book is an ideal introduction to the various branches of horsemanship. Whether you ride yourself or simply enjoy horses from the sidelines, here is a guide that will increase your enjoyment of the colourful world of horses.

Contents

Chapter one
Horses in the Wild

The first horse evolved about 60 million years ago, and was no larger than a medium-sized dog. Today, horses are found in every size and colour. Few other animals can compete with them for grace and beauty.

Horses and ponies, like all living creatures, including human beings, evolved over millions of years from the earliest forms of life which existed on the Earth. We are all, therefore, related to one another to some degree. In fact, if you compare the skeleton of a horse standing upright on its hindlegs with that of a man, you will see that the bone structure is quite similar.

We know about the early ancestor of the horse from remains discovered by scientists. Some of these remains were remarkably complete. The first bones and some portions of skull were found at Studd Hill in Kent, England, in 1839. They were so different from the equine (or horse-like) anatomy with which the scientists were familiar that Richard Owen, one of the greatest experts of the day, thought they belonged to an entirely different family. He named this early creature *Hyracotherium*, which implies membership of the rabbit family. The name *Hyracotherium*, although based on a false assumption, is still the name used in scientific circles.

Discovery of the Dawn Horse
Some years later, in 1876, a much more complete skeleton was found in America and the scientists were able to say conclusively that it belonged to the horse family. They called this animal *Eohippus,* which in Greek means Dawn Horse, a much more romantic and descriptive name for the early ancestor of what was to be one of the world's most important species. Scientists estimated that

Left: Young foals play together. *Right:* The Asiatic Wild Horse is one of the original three types from which all modern horses are thought to have descended. This primitive specimen is also known as the Przewalskii horse after the explorer who discovered wild herds in Mongolia in 1881. The Przewalskii has been hunted almost to extinction and it exists now only in zoos.

Eohippus had lived about 60 million years ago. They were able to show that the creature had evolved from an extinct group of animals of the *condylarth* family. More importantly they were able to trace the evolution of the horse as we know it (or nearly as we know it) from this primitive animal.

The modern horse, which we call *Equus caballus,* emerged about one million years ago on the American continent. *Equus caballus* was very different in appearance from *Eohippus* and quite a lot bigger.

We know, from remains like those found at Studd Hill, that *Eohippus* inhabited Western Europe, the Middle East and Asia, as well as North America. It was able to spread to all those parts of the world because before the Ice Ages the continents were joined together by bridges of land.

For some reason which we shall never know about, the various forms of *Eohippus* (and there were numerous variations on the basic theme)

An Exmoor pony mare with her foal. This breed is easily distinguished by the characteristic 'mealy' muzzle. It has a particularly tough and thick coat as protection against winter on Exmoor.

disappeared from Europe, as well as from Asia, some 40 million years ago, in the early part of the Oligocene period. The evolution of *Equus caballus* was, therefore, left to the varieties inhabiting the North American continent.

The Evolution of *Eohippus*
All animals have adapted themselves to their environments. Without the presence of man, the environment is the most important factor in evolution. Changes in the environment result in changes in the species inhabiting it and, even today, the environment changes slowly but constantly.

If, for instance, a group of Arab horses were to be run loose on mountain and moorland areas, over a period of time, significant changes would occur in the

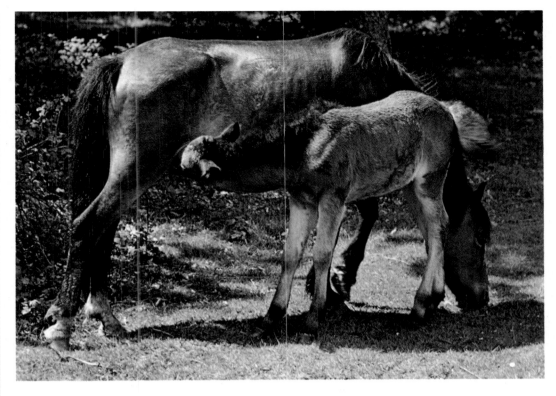

Left: This picture shows the second of the original 'primitive' types, the Tarpan, which used to inhabit large parts of Eastern Europe and the Ukrainian steppes. It too is now extinct in the wild but survives in a specially kept herd at Popielno in Poland. *Above:* A New Forest foal drinks from its dam (mother). Large herds of these ponies still run out in the New Forest in England.

descendants of the original group. Because of the scarcity of food the horses would not grow as large and would convert the available food more efficiently into what they needed within their bodies. They would, to give a very simple example, grow very much thicker coats in the winter than previously, so as to withstand the rigours of the climate. Their action, or the way they move, would also change. Instead of the low, floating movement so suited to travelling over flat, desert places, their movement would become higher and shorter. The knees would be increasingly bent so that the feet avoided tripping over the tussocks and stones which form rough mountain and moorland terrain.

Eohippus was the product of millions of years of evolution. It was almost another 60 million years before the modern horse, *Equus caballus,* was established on the Earth.

Although *Eohippus* is recognized as the first ancestor, it did not look very much like a modern horse. The reconstructions made by scientists suggest that the animal was about the size of a fox or a middle-size dog like a Labrador. The feet of *Eohippus* were more like those of a dog than a horse. The forefeet had four toes and the back

ones three. Each foot had a pad, like a dog, behind the toes. The head, the arrangement of the teeth and the position of the eyes, were also very different. The eyes were placed in the middle of the head and the jaws were formed to suit the needs of a browsing creature whose main diet was soft leaves—there was then no grass growing on the earth!

The process of evolution which followed was, of course, enormously complex. Hundreds of varieties of *Eohippus* must have existed, some bigger, some smaller, some more advanced and others less so, before the predominant strains leading to the single-hooved horse emerged. In very general terms, it is possible to trace the main stages of development.

After *Eohippus*
Eohippus, within the Eocene period which ended some 35 million years ago, was succeeded by *Orohippus* and *Epihippus.* These animals had stronger jaws and were therefore able to feed off a greater variety of foliage.

After them, in the Oligocene period (35–25 million years ago) came *Mesohippus* and *Miohippus.* Their teeth were an improvement again on those of their predecessors. They were able to cope with most of the types of soft vegetation growing in the environment of wooded scrub in which they lived. The ground over which they moved was still soft enough to require a padded foot, but in these animals the number of toes had been reduced to three on both front and hind feet and the weight was being borne increasingly on the central toe of each foot.

Significantly, the structure of the leg altered. It became longer and more powerful, and as a result the animal could move more quickly and at paces something like those of the modern horse. Because of the greater variety and availability of food the size increased also. *Mesohippus* was probably twice the size of *Eohippus*.

In the Miocene period, 25 million years ago, grasslands developed on the American continents. This added further impetus to the development of the species. The principal branch of the horse family in this period is called

Merychippus, the first of the grazing animals. Great changes occurred in the teeth, so that they could cope with hard grasses. The neck grew longer to make grazing easier and so that the head could be raised high enough to make maximum use of the horse's all-round vision. This was the first line of defence against meat-eating predators for herbivorous animals grazing in open country.

Although the lateral toes, much reduced in size, remained, the pad on the feet disappeared and the leg was much more like that of a modern horse.

The white horses of the Camargue—an ancient breed that inhabits the harsh marshlands of the Rhone delta in southern France. These horses are used by the *gardien* to herd the Camargue's black bulls.

Merychippus was probably about 10 hh (or 10 hands high, a hand being four inches, [102 mm]) and in him we can see the characteristics of the modern horse emerging. The more open grasslands made the animal an easier prey for predators. Because of this these early members of the horse family had to

develop good defences. Their increasingly long legs gave them the ability to run from their enemies. The senses of smell and hearing which warned them of danger were also heightened. These characteristics are still very much part of the highly-strung nature of the modern horse. Its immediate reaction to danger, or even to suspected danger, is always to run away as fast as possible.

The arrival of *Equus caballus*
Some six million years ago the first single-hooved animal, *Pliohippus*, had

evolved and from this final prototype came *Equus caballus*. The species *Equus* spread from the North American continent through Asia into Africa and Europe. After the Ice Ages, which removed the remaining land bridges between the Old and New Worlds, four closely related types of *Equus* survived: the horse, the ass, the zebra and the onager. Horses were to be found in Europe and parts of Asia; onagers lived in the Middle East, and zebras and asses inhabited the north and south of Africa, respectively.

By this time *Equus caballus* had

reached about 13 hh. The only physical characteristic in common with his early ancestors was the ergot on the point of the heel—all that was left of the last toe.

Then occurred one of the world's great and so far unsolved mysteries. For some reason, a fatal disease perhaps, the horse became extinct in North America, the place of its birth. The Americas were by then cut off from the other continents, and so isolated from the rest of the world.

This happened about 8,000 years ago. No horses trod on American soil again until 1511 when the Spanish

11

conquistadore, Hernan Cortes, took 16 horses with him to Havana, Cuba, in preparation for his invasion of Mexico.

In the rest of the world, horses continued to develop according to the dictates of their environment. Mild climates combined with a generous growth of suitable herbage produced larger animals. Harsh climates, often found in mountainous regions where vegetation was sparse, resulted in hardy ponies. Dry regions tended to produce light-boned, fast-moving animals. Areas of high rainfall and lush vegetation encouraged heavier, slower animals.

The modern horse

After the Ice Ages the horse population seems to have divided into three distinct types, from which all our modern horses descend.

In Asia there was the Steppe Horse, known also as the Asiatic Wild Horse or as Przewalskii's horse, after the Russian colonel who discovered a wild herd in Mongolia in 1881. The full name of this horse, is *Equus przewalskii przewalskii* Poliakov. It is now extinct in the wild but is preserved in a number of zoos.

The second type was the Plateau Horse, which is known as the Tarpan (*Equus przewalskii gmelini* Antonius). It inhabited large areas of Eastern Europe and the Ukrainian steppes. This horse, too, was hunted until it was to all practical purposes extinct. It survives in a herd kept at Popielno in Poland, but it is doubtful whether this is the original horse or a very near 'man-made' replica.

Finally, there was the Forest or Diluvial Horse, a massive, slow-moving animal inhabiting the wet pasturelands of northern Europe. This horse is now certainly extinct.

It is believed that the Przewalskii and the Tarpan are the direct ancestors of all the light horse population of the world, while the Forest is responsible for the great heavy horse breeds.

Hippologists (people who make a study of horses—*hippos* is the Greek word for horse) differentiate between the light and heavy horses. They call light horses 'warm-bloods' and heavy horses 'cold-bloods.' These terms do not, however, refer to the body temperature. They mean that light horses have Eastern blood in them, by which is meant Arabian and Thoroughbred, while heavy horses have nothing of these breeds in their make-up.

The Przewalskii horse has an average height of about 13 hh. It is notable for its short, upright mane and sparsely covered tail which is tufted at the top and bottom. The colour is a sand-dun with black legs, mane and tail and a cream underbelly.

The Tarpan is the same height but is a much more refined specimen with a lighter, less 'primitive' head. It is distinguished by its blue-dun colour and the eel stripe (a dark band) running

A Welsh Pony mare on the moorlands of her native land. The very beautiful Welsh Pony is one of the most popular of all the pony breeds and is in great demand as a high-class riding pony. Formerly it was used for shepherding on the Welsh hills and it still retains the hereditary characteristics of soundness and hardiness.

Shetland ponies are an ancient breed originating in the Shetland and Orkney Islands. Although standing only 38–42 in (97–107 cm) high at the top of the shoulder the little Shetland is the strongest of all horses in comparison to its size. The harsh environment of the Islands and the scarcity of food is responsible for the breed's small stature and incredible toughness. Shetlands were originally bred for farm work.

down the length of the back.

We do not know exactly how the Forest Horse looked but we can make an informed guess. Scientists can reconstruct these early horses from excavated remains—some found in Scandinavia are estimated as being 10,000 years old. There is also the evidence of paintings drawn on the walls of cave dwellings by primitive man.

The Forest Horse would have been over 15 hh, massively bodied, with thick legs and broad, flat feet to cope with the swamp conditions in which it lived. The manes and tails were long and thick, as was the coarse hair covering the body in winter. The horses were usually bay, brown or black, colours which blended well with the dark, forest background.

Wild horses today

Sadly, there are no true 'wild' horses left, unless one counts the 'brumbies' of Australia and the 'mustangs' of America. Both these are really domestic horses that have reverted to the wild state.

There are, however, horses living in herds just as their ancestors did. The horses of the Camargue in southern France are one example. In Britain there are herds of Exmoor ponies, Welsh ponies and New Forests all living in their native habitats. Dominant stallions keep together their bands of mares, mark their territories and lead their groups from one grazing area to the other, just as their wild ancestors would have done. The foals, already equipped at birth with long legs, follow the herd within hours of being born, as indeed they have always done.

The British native breeds are particularly well-suited to their environment, being hardy and sound and well able to exist on sparse feed. The characteristics of these 'wild' herds are a result of their environment. The modern domestic horse is as much the result of human intervention. As soon as early tribesmen tamed horses for their own use, they also started to choose the horses from which to breed new stock. This is a process which has continued and has helped to produce the huge variety of breeds we have today.

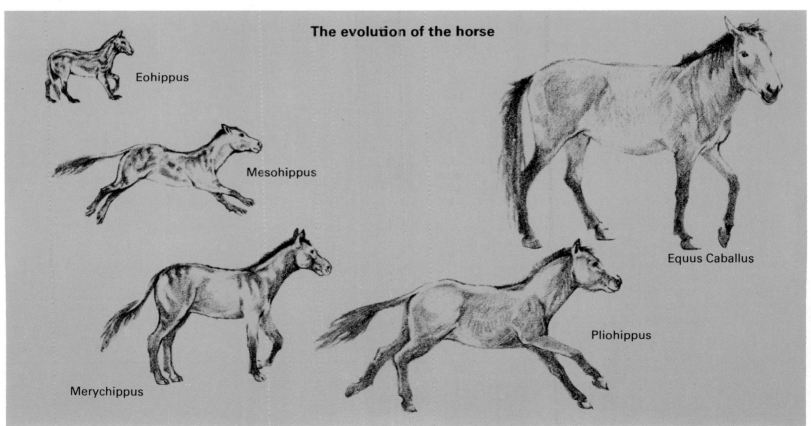

The evolution of the horse

Eohippus

Mesohippus

Merychippus

Pliohippus

Equus Caballus

Chapter two
Horses round the World

As soon as we realized how useful horses could be to us, we tried to improve on nature. Careful breeding improved strength or speed. Today there are some 200 different breeds of horse scattered round the world.

The environment was certainly responsible for the early evolution of the horse. However the subsequent development of the species, over the past 4,000 years or so at any rate, has been very much influenced by man's constant efforts to improve upon what nature provided. Once the horse was domesticated, and men began to understand how horses could be used to help them in their lives, the development of the horse was accelerated in a remarkable way. Improved methods of agriculture and crop management resulted in the production of greater quantities of high-nutrition feedstuffs. By selective breeding, and cross-breeding between specific groups, men were able to produce bigger horses, stronger horses and faster ones according to their particular needs. Usually the principal need was to produce a good war horse. Of course, they never managed to produce the *perfect* horse for a particular purpose, but human nature is such that they went on trying—and we are still trying today!

We do not know for certain exactly when horses were first domesticated. It seems likely, from the evidence that exists, that it was at some time between 3,000–2,000 BC. The people concerned were probably tribes of tough Indo-Europeans living on the steppes, north of the mountain ranges bordering the Black and Caspian Seas.

Men, of course, had made use of horses long before this date, hunting them for food and for their skins. In the early days of domestication the motives for keeping herds of horses were probably similar. The horses provided an easily available source of fresh meat, the mares could be milked, hides could be

A Lipizzaner stallion of the famous Spanish Riding School in Vienna, performing the *levade*. This is an example of one of the classical movements of High School riding.

used to make clothes and shelters and even the dung, when dried, had its use—it was good fuel for fires. Even today in Mongolia and in huge areas of the USSR herds of horses are kept for exactly those purposes. The animals are bred specifically to increase their milk yields and also the weight of their carcases for meat.

Later, horses were used as pack animals or to pull loads carried on simple platforms of poles, such as the *travois* of the American Indian. This consisted of poles tied together in an 'A' shape and dragged along the ground behind the horse. It was only much later that horses were ridden. Both reindeers and, in the Middle East, onagers were ridden long before horses.

The first evidence of horses being used in war was to pull chariots. Chariot racing was featured at the 25th Olympiad held in 680 BC. Ridden races were introduced about 40 years later but they were not generally accepted until the Games of 256 BC.

The saddle and the stirrup

Perhaps one of the first of the great horse-people were the warlike Assyrians (890–824 BC). They used horses with chariots as well as for riding. Although they had neither saddle nor stirrup they hunted lions with bow and arrow from horseback.

Saddles were not in general use until the fourth century AD when they were introduced by the Sarmatians. A century later the stirrup came out of Mongolia with the Huns of Atilla and was introduced into Europe.

These two inventions, and particularly the stirrup, were of enormous importance. It might even be said that they played a significant part in shaping the world's history. In the first place they made the mounted soldier much more mobile. With the help of a saddle and stirrups he was able to cover longer distances at faster speeds and with less

A grey Shire horse enjoying a holiday at grass. The Shires, the most powerful horses in the world, are still used in agriculture and for heavy haulage in towns and cities.

tiredness. Secondly, and very importantly, it altered the role of the cavalry soldier. Previously, because they could be so easily unseated, cavalrymen had been unable to fight hand to hand with bodies of enemy foot soldiers. With saddle and stirrups, the rider could stay firmly on his horse's back. The cavalry could now charge bodies of infantry with lance and sword. Thus the mounted soldier became a very effective weapon of war. The new role of the cavalry had a decisive effect upon the development of the war horse.

Eastern horsemen continued to use a fast, light horse for, indeed, they had none other. In Europe in the Middle Ages the move was gradually towards the Great Horse. It was capable of carrying the weight of its armoured rider, and was bred from the descendants of the primitive Forest Horse. However, this move was gradual. The mounted knight of the history books did not, at first wear a suit of plate armour. Nor did he ride a Great Horse. Instead he wore light chain mail and sat on an Arab-type horse. A good example is found in the knights who landed with William the Conqueror at Hastings in 1066. William's knights when fully equipped weighed an average of 224 lb (102 kg), while a cavalryman in the First World War weighed between 280–288 lb (111–114 kg) in marching order!

Knights in chain mail dominated the battlefields of Europe for many years. The change to Great Horses and heavy plate armour was forced on them by the increasing use of the longbow.

At Crècy, in 1346, companies of Welsh bowmen, stationed on the wings of the English army, cut to pieces the cream of French chivalry with whistling hordes of expertly directed arrows. Thereafter horse and rider needed the protection of increasingly heavy armour, and horses had to be big enough to carry the weight. The swift cavalry charge of the soldier clad in chain mail was reduced to a thunderous but infinitely ponderous trot. The knight and his horse were little more than a very slowly moving fortress of iron and steel.

The changes in the role of the mounted knight also led to changes in the art of equitation. Since the knight carried his weapon in his right hand, he held the reins in his left; this hand also bore his shield, so it had to be held high. The horse was controlled with a curb bit of monstrous proportions but neck-reining was also practised. The horses were well trained to obey the long-spurred heels. The means by which the big horses were controlled seem savage to us, and depended almost entirely on mechanical devices. However, there is no doubt that the knights were exceptionally skilful in controlling their horses. What is more, it is to them that we owe the discipline of classical riding. It survives today in the soaring leaps above the ground, the *pirouettes* and *levades* practised so expertly at the Spanish Riding School at Vienna and by the French Cadre Noir at Saumur.

Riding as an art

The period between AD 1500 and 1600 is the *Renaissance*. The word means 're-birth' and it was the time when the world entered into an era of culture such as had never before been experienced. The arts of music, painting, sculpture and poetry flourished and flowered and there was a surge of enthusiastic interest in science, mathematics and architecture. The noblemen of Europe vied with each other as classical scholars and also as *horsemen*—for the art of riding was considered as much a part of a gentleman's education as a knowledge of Latin and Greek.

Throughout Europe, and particularly in Italy, riding halls of baroque magnificence were built. Young men rode the exercises which had originated with the mounted knight in press of battle! The leaps, like the *capriole* and *courbette,* were used in battle to deter enemy infantry. The lashing hindlegs incapacitated any enemy who tried to attack from the rear. The pirouette was a necessary manoeuvre to enable the sword arm to be used to best effect. The lofty *passage* and *piaffe* exactly suited the victor in his moment of triumph.

The Spanish Riding School was founded during this period, in 1572. It was so called because it was founded on horses imported from Spain. The most notable importation was made in 1580 when nine stallions and 24 mares were taken from Spain to Lipizza at the command of the Archduke Charles of Austria. Their descendants, with a later infusion of Arab blood, are the white Lipizzaners of the modern Spanish School in Vienna.

The Andalucian

This Spanish horse, later and presently known as the Andalucian, was until the end of the 18th century the foremost horse in Europe. It was the mount of every crowned head of state and its influence was enormous. Spanish horses went with the *conquistadores* to America and re-established the horse on that continent. Many of the great carriage and riding breeds of Europe were either founded on the Andalucian or owed much to the breed.

The Andalucian is essentially a noble horse of great presence. He has an unusually impressive front with a strong, proudly curved neck supporting a head that is almost hawk-like in profile. The mane and tail is wavy and extravagant. The movement, particularly with the forelegs, is high, showy and exaggerated. The Andalucian is no galloper, nor does it jump very effectively, but it is strong and agile and a superb horse for dressage and High School riding. Today, in Spain, it is favoured as a parade horse for the *feria* (fairs) and as the courageous mount of the *rejoneadore,* the mounted bullfighter. How the breed evolved is not known for certain. It seems likely that Muslim invaders of the Iberian Peninsula brought with them eastern horses of some kind. They are more likely to have been North African Barbs than Arabians. These were crossed with the horses indigenous to the area eventually giving rise to the Andalucian.

The Arabian

The importance of the Spanish Horse in equestrian history is undeniable. However it is outclassed entirely by the contribution made to the world horse population by the oldest and most pure of all the horse breeds, the Arabian.

Of the early origins of this beautiful horse we know little, and what facts exist are often obscured in myth and legend—for no horse evokes such

A beautiful study of a Lipizzaner in his stable. The Lipizzaner, though full of courage, has a wonderfully gentle temperament. The breed is also long-lived, often working until over 20 years.

Arabian mares and foals in contrasting environments. Those on the left belong to a famous Swedish stud, while those below are at Bahrain in the country in which the breed originated.

uncritical adulation and none is more romantic.

It seems possible, however, that a superlative breed of horse inhabited the Arabian peninsula as long ago as 5,000 BC, when that part of the world was not a desert but a green and fertile land. Early Egyptian monuments, and in particular a statuette, dated between 2,000 and 1,300 BC show horses with pronounced Arabian characteristics.

Unravelling the early history of the Arabian horse is made even more difficult by the lack of written or pictorial information. The desert tribes passed on

The Arabian horse is the most ancient and the purest of all the horse breeds. It is first and foremost a riding horse of the highest quality and is perfectly suited to be the mount of Morocco's *Garde Royale,* seen above in the grounds of the king's palace at Rabat. Although the Arabian originated in the deserts of Arabia the breed is to be found all over the world.

pedigrees by word of mouth from father to son, and both the Muslim and Hebrew religions forbade the making or keeping of pictures and statues.

There is, however, one notable Arab historian, El Kelbi (AD 786). He traced the pedigrees of the Arab horses to those which ran wild in the Yemen in the time of Bax, the great-great-grandson of Noah. Bax tamed the Yemeni horses and El Kelbi's pedigrees go back to two foundation horses, the stallion Hoshaba

and the mare Baz.

This may be legend or history. There is no doubt, however, that there was a very ancient race of horses native to the Arabian peninsula. Once they spread outwards from their desert homelands, their influence on the breeds with which they came in contact was enormous.

The worth of the Arabian horse was known in Europe in very early times, but it was not until the era of the Prophet Mohammed that the effect of crossing the Arab with native stock of lesser quality began to be felt.

Mohammed was a politician and a soldier as well as a religious leader. He made sure of an adequate supply of cavalry by incorporating the care of the horse into the demands of the Muslim faith. The welfare of the horse became a religious duty for the fierce, desert warriors. As a result the horse herds increased in number and in quality.

Mohammed died in AD 632 just as the Muslim forces began the campaign which led to their occupation of lands far outside their desert kingdoms. They overran the Middle East, established themselves firmly in the Iberian Peninsula and pressed onwards as far as Touraine in France. There they remained for more than a hundred years. All that time the Arab horses they brought with them bred with the native horses of the occupied territories. Gradually the Arab influence spread even beyond these boundaries into the rest of Europe.

This influence would not, however, have survived had not the Arab been a very special horse indeed. It was superior in stamina, speed and prepotency (the power to transmit hereditary qualities) to every other breed with which it came into contact.

In height the Arab is a small horse,

Left: A desert-bred Arabian stallion wearing the typical neck decoration of the desert tribes. The wide, flared nostrils, the large eye and the alert, shapely ears are prized characteristics of the breed. *Right:* A Thoroughbred mare and her foal. The Thoroughbred is descended directly from Arab sires imported into England in the 17th and 18th centuries.

usually a little under 15 hh, but it is always a 'horse' and never referred to as a 'pony'. In appearance the breed is unique, being marked by the fine head, 'dished' face and huge wide-set eyes. The carriage of the horse is regal and the tail is carried upwards like a banner. The Arab is unique, too, in its physical structure. It has 17 ribs, five lumbar bones and 16 tail vertebrae as opposed to the 18-6-18 formation usual in other horses.

Some 200 breeds and types make up the world population of horses. Scarcely more than a handful of these have not at some time benefited from infusions of Arab blood. Nearly all the British native pony breeds have been improved by Arab crosses. The French Anglo-Arab is a direct Arab horse derivative, and is the product of crosses between the pure-bred Arab and the Thoroughbred.

The Thoroughbred

The Thoroughbred is perhaps the greatest horse produced out of Arab blood. The Thoroughbred breed was founded in England by three famous Arab stallions: the Byerley Turk (imported in 1689), the Darley Arabian (imported in 1704) and the Godolphin Arabian (imported in 1728). All Thoroughbred horses throughout the world trace their descent from one or other of these founding fathers.

In its turn the Thoroughbred, the fastest and most highly developed horse in the world, has had an influence almost equal to the Arab. It has been used extensively to give greater size, speed, courage and quality to other breeds. Today, horse-breeding throughout the world is based on the Arab and its larger and faster derivative, the Thoroughbred.

In high-level competitive events the Arab is no match for the Thoroughbred or part-Thoroughbred. Arab horses are not big enough to jump the formidable fences built in show-jumping rings and on cross-country courses. The Arab does not seem to be acceptable as a dressage horse as judges and competitors seem to prefer heavier, more powerful German-type horses. The Arab is also far too slow for racing, at least in comparison with the Thoroughbred.

The development of dressage
Modern dressage has its roots in the movements performed in battle by the armoured Knights of the Middle Ages. These gave birth to the classical riding of the Renaissance, upon which much of the work of the Spanish School is founded.

Armoured knight

'High school' rider

Modern dressage rider

On the other hand Arabs are virtually impossible to better in the sport of long-distance riding. They are tougher than other horses, inherently sound and possess enormous stamina and weight-carrying ability. It was for these qualities, as well as because of the Arab's gentle and easily managed nature, that they were used in cavalry regiments all over the world well into the 19th century.

Arab enthusiasts still insist that the Arab is the world's most perfect riding horse because of the supreme comfort of his floating paces. And the Arab is still just as much in demand as ever. Huge numbers are bred in the United States, which has the biggest Arab horse population in the world. No less than 10,000 foals are registered in California each year alone. Britain, another stronghold of Arab breeding, has some 900 privately owned studs and there are vast state-owned Arabian studs in Poland, Hungary, Germany and France.

The heavy horses

And what of the Great War Horses of Europe? They descended from the primitive, cold-blooded Forest Horse of Northern Europe. They were developed in the Middle Ages to carry armoured knights, who were the equivalent of today's heavy tank brigades. Later, their main use was pulling the heavily built coaches necessary for the appalling roads of the period. These were deeply rutted in summer and muddy quagmires in winter. Once roads were tarred, lighter vehicles could be used, drawn by lighter and faster horses. In Britain a network of tarred roads only came into being by the middle of the 19th century. In continental Europe, it was even longer before good roads became a reality.

In the towns and cities, heavy horses were responsible for the haulage of goods. When systems of waterways were built it was again heavy horses which provided the power to move the loaded barges. These barge horses developed quite extraordinary skills, learning to jump stiles on the towpaths, how to cross the canal from one side to another by jumping on and off the barge, and coping with the intricacies of the locks.

Up to the end of the 19th century and the development of the internal combustion engine, Europe's agricultural economy depended upon horse-power. All the farm work from ploughing, harvesting and threshing to general carting jobs was done by horses. This state of affairs continued well into the 20th century and in some European countries horses are still a common sight.

This dependence on heavy working

Above: Austria's distinctive Haflinger pony is used for all sorts of farm work. Tough and hardy, the breed does not exceed 14.2 hh and is always chestnut in colour with flaxen manes and tails.

Below: These heavy cart horses may stand as much as 18 hh and weigh as much as a ton. In Canada and Australia, as well as parts of Europe, horses like these are used for hauling timber.

horses led to interesting differences in the types bred from one country to another, and in the various areas of those countries. Work horses in mountainous regions, like the Austrian Haflingers, were closer to ponies in appearance. They were far lighter than the huge horses such as the Shires, Boulonnais and Ardennes which were developed for their ability to work on heavy soil. Lighter soils called for lighter, more active horses, such as the Polish, Finnish and some of the Russian breeds. The Clydesdale, the very popular Scottish heavy horse, was much used for

urban transport and was developed as an active heavy horse with a longer and freer stride than is usual in the draught breeds.

The numbers of heavy horses naturally declined as their place was taken by petrol and diesel-driven vehicles. However, in recent years, there has been a revival of interest in the heavy horse. Brewers are extending their use of horse transport and there is a move towards greater use of horses in agriculture, particularly on farms with small acreage.

In Britain there are four heavy

A pair of English Shires at work with the plough. Their bridles and martingales are decorated with horse-brasses of various designs. These used to be considered as charms against evil—part of the 'horseman's lore'.

breeds—the Shire, Clydesdale, Suffolk Punch and Percheron. All four have thriving breed societies and can report steady and significant increases in the registration of youngstock. Heavy horse classes are a feature of the major shows and there are special shows held annually for all four breeds.

Chapter three
The Horse in North America

The birthplace of the horse, millions of years ago, was North America. Horses played a vital part in the history of the United States, and today they have a special place in the hearts of many Americans.

When the first Spanish *conquistadores* landed on the American continent in the early part of the 16th century they found no horses at all. The history of the horse in America, therefore, so far as any modern study is concerned, spans only 400 years or so. In terms of history this represents no more than the flicker of an eyelid.

It is remarkable that within such a short space of time, the United States have acquired an equestrian culture and a horse population that in colour and variety can hardly be exceeded elsewhere in the world.

Another fascinating thought is that within something less than 200 years a pioneering colony was able to become a world power—an achievement that would have been difficult without the help of horses.

Indian horses

The early Spanish explorers made their conquests because the native population had never before seen horses, and was terrified by the sight of mounted men. 'Next to God,' said Cortes, 'we owed our victory to the horses.'

A century after Cortes landed in Mexico, horses had spread northwards and had revolutionized the lives of the Plains Indians. They acquired the 'big dogs', as they called them, by trading, stealing and rounding up strays. Horses gave new mobility to the Indian tribes. Those tribes which had formerly led a settled existence in their villages abandoned the primitive tools used to till the ground and became hunters. The nomadic peoples, like the Blackfoot, Comanche, Kiowa and Apache found that horses gave them an easier and more prosperous life.

Mustangs are still to be found in parts of the United States and Canada. These semi-wild horses descend from those brought to the New World by the 16th-century Spanish *conquistadores*.

The American Indians soon adapted to the role of horse-people. They quickly evolved their own sort of saddlery. Their saddles were made from animal skins stuffed with grasses and kept in place by an arrangement of thongs. They made stirrups from cottonwood and poplar which they bent to the required shape and covered with rawhide. For a 'war bridle', the most common type in use, they used a piece of braided rawhide. This was tied round the horse's lower jaw and the two free ends served as reins. Horses were also used for transport. They were either pack-loaded or harnessed to the ingenious *travois* to carry the lodge, or tent, and all the family possessions of pots, skins etc. A *travois* was made of two poles, often the lodge poles, tied to form an A-shape and hitched one each side of the horse. A platform of thongs was made between the poles behind the horse, on which baggage was loaded and the pole ends just dragged along the ground. Much use

The United States has a great variety of colourful breeds and types of horses. The top picture is of a group of pintos or 'painted' horses, once very popular with the American Indian tribes. They are still bred in America, as is the spotted Appaloosa, above.

was made of horses for raiding and for war and, of course, for hunting buffalo. The Indian economy depended on the buffalo for it provided food, clothing and shelter for the tribes. Racing, too, was a popular leisure pursuit among the Indians. Races were held over distances of two to four miles (1·2–2·4 km) and horses were kept specially for this sport.

The Indian horses, which came from Spanish stock, were tough, wiry animals, standing not much more than 14 hh. They were small because of inbreeding, hard usage and small food rations. Coloured horses, pintos, Palominos and those with spotted coat patterns, were much prized and some of the tribes

practised selective breeding. They gelded, or castrated, the colts not considered to be good enough for breeding stock.

The Appaloosa
The best known of the Indian horses were the strikingly spotted Appaloosas, and they still *exist* as a breed today. These horses, in fact, represent the spotted strain which was once common in their ancestor the Spanish horse, but which is no longer seen in the present day Andalucian. The spotted horse is of very ancient origin and horses of similar markings and characteristics can be seen in early Chinese and Persian art. Originally, spotted horses must have come to Spain from Central Asia. They reached their American home in the Palouse Valley of Idaho from Mexico. The Palouse Valley was part of the tribal

lands of the Nez Perce Indians, and the name Appaloosa is a corruption of Palouse or Palousy.

Although Appaloosas are usually thought of as being spotted, and most do have a spotted coat pattern of one sort or another, they do not *have* to be spotted. An Appaloosa can be a whole flecked roan colour without spots. But even unspotted Appaloosas have the other distinctive characteristics of the breed. The eye is always circled, like a human eye, with a white sclera; the skin on the nose, lips and between the hindlegs is a mottled pink and the hooves are marked with vertical black and white stripes. Usually the hair of the mane and tail is sparse and wispy.

There are six recognized coat patterns for Appaloosas, which are virtually self-explanatory. They are: leopard, snowflake, marble (the whole roan

The re-establishment of the horse on the American continent changed the way of life of the Plains Indians. Formerly nomadic farmers, they became horsemen and hunters of buffalo.

colour), frost, spotted, blanket and white blanket.

All spotted horses are not, of course, Appaloosas. The name applies only to those horses registered with the American Appaloosa Society and its British counterpart. There are other spotted strains to be found in Europe. Denmark has a spotted breed of its own called the Knabstrup.

Ponies in America
In general terms America does not have a native pony population, although there are a great number of British native ponies, such as the Welsh, Connemara,

Dartmoor, New Forest etc., which have been imported into the United States.

So-called 'wild' ponies can still be found on the islands of Chincoteague and Assateague, off the coast of Virginia and Maryland, but these are really stunted horses. The nearest thing to a native pony is the Pony of the Americas. This is a breed which was created in a very short space of time by a man called Leslie Boomhower of Mason City, Iowa. He crossed a Shetland pony stallion with an Appaloosa mare and produced miniatures of the famous spotted breed. The ponies stand between 11·2 hh and 13 hh and must have the characteristic Appaloosa markings.

A rather less successful attempt to produce an American pony is represented by the American Shetland. This is very like a Hackney pony with the same high, harness action. It was created by crossing Scottish Shetlands with Hackney ponies and then adding a little Arab blood and a cash of Thoroughbred. The result is interesting but nothing like the tough, rough-coated little Shetland of the north of Scotland.

Riding Western style

The Europeans who pioneered their way across the continent to win the West brought many sorts of horses with them. They also used those they found in the country, which were similar to the ones ridden by the Indian tribes. As cattle-rearing became established in the West so there was a need for a mounted cowman, or cowboy, to move and generally watch over the huge herds. The cattle lands, for the most part, bordered on Mexico which had strong Spanish connections. It was not surprising, therefore, that the cowboy should adopt equipment, which with local variations and some odd additions, had been introduced by the Spaniards who had settled in Mexico.

The cowboy or Western saddle is to all intents and purposes the saddle of Spain. Even today there is little difference between the two, apart from the roping horn on the Western saddle. In turn, the Spanish saddle has its origin in the high-peaked saddle of the Muslim invaders who occupied Spain in the seventh century! Similarly, the method of schooling and breaking is well known in Spain where it originates. The *bosal,* a weighted noseband, is used first. Then follows the hackamore (*jacquima*—a bitless bridle), and finally the long-cheeked spade bit, which is commonplace in California. Less surprisingly, the style and method of riding employed by the Californian cowboy is similar to that used by his counterpart in Spain as he tends the fierce black bulls of Andalucia. Even their dress is much the same—boots and spurs are pretty well identical, both wear chaps, or *chaperos,* and their hats are similar.

The cowboy way of life gave rise to a number of sporting events which reflected the cowboy's job. These sports now make up the programme at the many highly popular rodeos which are held all over the West. Principal events at the rodeos are 'bronco' riding, barrel racing, steer-roping, bulldogging, chuck wagon racing and so on. These are all very tough sports and the competitors, male and female, have to be very tough characters.

Western riding is just as skilful, if not more so, than the conventional riding practised in Europe. The Western saddle and the seat adopted is not suitable for jumping, but the cowboy saddle is very comfortable for both horse and rider when covering long distances. In the very tough, competitive long-distance rides held in America and Australia many competitors 'ride Western'. Although the Western saddle is heavy in comparison with the usual European saddle it has the advantage of spreading the weight of

Above: A good example of an Appaloosa in working gear. The long-cheeked bit may look very severe, but in a trained horse this is not the case as the horse is ridden on a 'looping', loose rein and changes of direction are made by neck-reining. *Left:* The powerful Quarter Horse is the world's best cow-pony. It got its name from the races run by early settlers over a quarter mile.

saddle and rider over a much larger area of the horse's back. The European saddle concentrates the weight over a relatively small part of the back.

The Western bridle with the long-cheeked 'spade' bit looks as if it is a very severe instrument, but this is not really so. Or, more correctly, it is not severe in the right hands. A good Western horseman rides with a looping rein, the only pressure on the horse's mouth coming from the weight on the rein. To slow the pace, or to stop, the Western horseman uses his legs, in the same way as the European rider, to get the horse's hindlegs engaged well under the body. Once the horse has been well balanced, the rider only has to raise his bridle hand to stop it. With a well-schooled Western horse, there is no need to put any pressure on the horse's mouth. Western riders frequently ride

a compact, chunky horse, very well-balanced and with enormously powerful quarters. This feature of the breed was developed because of the type of racing for which the horses were used. The first racetracks were either a rough pathway hacked out of the forest, or just the length of a village street. Neither was much more than 440 yards (402 m) long, or a 'quarter' mile—hence the breed name Quarter Horse. Although used for all sorts of work, the Quarter Horse raced over these tracks at extraordinary speeds largely because its very powerful quarters allowed it to get into full gallop within a stride or two of the start.

Once proper courses were built, the Quarter Horse moved into the West with the white settlers to become the world's best cow pony. Today, however, Quarter Horse racing is very popular again and offers big prize money.

Left: A splendid example of a pinto, 'painted', stallion. Coloured horses, like this one, were popular with the American Indians because the broken colour pattern provided good camouflage. Pintos have a reputation for toughness and endurance.
Below: A 20th-century cowboy rounds up a bunch of cow-ponies.

using only one hand and Western horses are schooled to turn by the neck-rein.

A fairly large number of riders in Europe, particularly those interested in distance riding, now use Western 'tack' (saddlery), and in Britain there is a flourishing Western Horseman's Association.

The American Quarter Horse

The best cattle horse in the world is the American Quarter Horse. In rodeos it quickly develops an uncanny 'cow-sense', working the cattle just like a sheep-dog, and often doing so quite independently of its rider. The Quarter Horse is claimed to be the most popular horse in the world, and since there are over one million of them officially registered the claim is well justified.

It is not, however, a 'Western' horse, as it was first bred and developed in the east among the colonial seaboard settlements of the Carolinas and Virginia. English colonists of the early 18th century imported racehorses (they were not then called Thoroughbreds) so that they could continue their favourite sport in their new country. They crossed the imported racehorses with good Spanish mares, and they also mated tough Spanish stallions with English racing mares. The result, in the end, was

The Morgan

Very much the 'all-American' horse is the Morgan which, like the Quarter Horse, is not big, standing about 15–15·2 hh.

All Morgans descend from one very special stallion. This was originally called Figure but is better known by the name of its second owner, Justin Morgan, the Vermont schoolteacher who acquired the horse in 1795.

Justin Morgan, the original stallion, was one of the most versatile animals in the whole history of horses. Although only 14 hh it ploughed and worked at clearing woodlands, hauling out huge stumps that no other horse could move.

The Morgan is one of America's best-known breeds and this mare and her foal are good examples.

It was matched endlessly in weight-pulling contests, and never lost one. It raced under saddle and in harness and was never beaten.

Today's Morgan is still a great all-rounder. It is a show and pleasure horse, goes well in harness and can still compete at weight-pulling.

Pacing and trotting

The United States is also the home of 'gaited' horses. They were once popular in Europe but are now no longer seen there. The gaited breeds developed from the plantation horses of the south. The best known of them is the Kentucky Saddler, the modern name of which is the American Saddle Horse. Originally the saddler was purely a utility horse, its gaits being developed to suit a variety of circumstances. It was also always a

striking and very showy animal. Today, Saddle Horses are used mainly in the show ring and come in three distinct types: the Three-gaited Saddle Horse, the Five-gaited and the Harness Horse.

The Three-gaited Saddle Horse is shown at walk, trot and canter, all of which are performed with great animation and with a high, exaggerated action. The Five-gaited Saddler has two more paces, the slow-gait and the rack. The slow-gait is a four-beat pace, executed with a very high action and a distinct moment of suspension in each footfall. The rack is the slow-gait carried out at full speed—which is very fast and spectacular.

Although the Saddle Horse is very popular in the United States, some people do not like the way it is shown or the methods used to obtain the unusual

paces. The feet on Saddlers are always grown very long and the tails are always 'nicked' to get the characteristic high tail carriage.

Another American horse in the same tradition is the next-door neighbour of the Saddle Horse, the Tennessee Walker. It is said to give the most comfortable ride in the world. The horse glides along very swiftly in a four-beat pace that is half walk and half run. There is no movement of the back to disturb the rider who can sit almost as comfortably as in an armchair. The Walker was another plantation horse. It was once called the 'Turn-Row' because it could be used to inspect crops, going up and down the rows without ever damaging the plants.

The third member of this gaited trio is the Missouri Fox Trotter, a lesser known breed originating in the Ozark Hills of Missouri. This horse is also claimed to be extremely comfortable. The gait in this instance is a 'broken' one, the horse walking energetically with the fore-feet and trotting behind.

In the United States the sport of trotting attracts crowds just as large as those which support flat racing or steeplechasing. It is not surprising, therefore, that America should have produced the fastest trotting breed in the world, the American Standardbred. It is made up of a number of lines but has a Thoroughbred horse as its principal foundation stallion. This was Messenger, born in 1780 and a direct descendant of the famous Darley Arabian.

The name Standardbred arises from the early practice of testing a horse's performance before it could be included in the official American Trotting Register. The 'standard' was 2 minutes 30 seconds over a mile for trotters and 2 minutes 25 seconds over the same distance for pacers. Trotters are those horses which trot conventionally by moving the legs in diagonal pairs. Pacers move their legs in lateral pairs.

The first sub two-minute mile was trotted in 1897 by a pacer called Star Pointer. Today, times under two minutes are quite often returned and records rarely stand for very long. The present 'standard' is 2 minutes 20 seconds.

Top: A cowboy at work on his well-trained cow-pony, probably a Quarter Horse, catches up a semi-wild mustang. *Below:* The cowboy at play in the rodeo event of bronco riding. The modern rodeo is a tough, professional sport, but its origins were in the day to day work of the cowboy, during which it was necessary to master rough horses; drive, herd and cut out cattle and so on.

The Narragansett Pacer

The Standardbred, the Saddle Horse, the Walking Horse and the Fox Trotter all share to some degree a common ancestor in a horse which is now extinct as a breed. This was the Narragansett Pacer. The Narragansett was founded on the 'ambling' horses which came to America from Britain. Ambling is the old English word for pacing, which was popular in Britain until the reign of King Charles II. Then racing took over, and the pacing, or ambling, breeds declined in popularity. In America they were crossed with Spanish stock (many of which had the pacing gait) to produce the Narragansett.

Unhappily the breed died out because of its own popularity. Planters in the West Indies needed such horses and bought the Narragansett in such quantities that in the end the breed ceased to exist. Now there is no trace of it in the West Indies either.

Above: A young rider in Western gear on a Palomino pony. Palominos, which are very popular as 'parade' horses in America, have coats the colour of 'a newly-minted gold coin' and pure white manes and tails. *Right:* The Tennessee Walker, which was developed on the plantations of the South, is one of the most unusual of the American breeds. It moves at a half-run, half-walk and is said to be the most comfortable ride in the world.

32

Western and European tack
Although there are marked differences between the Western saddle and that used in Europe and on the East coast of America, both trace their origin to the dip-seated saddle of the mounted warrior.

The European all-purpose saddle is probably the most popular of all.

Western horses are trained in hackamore, or bitless, bridles.

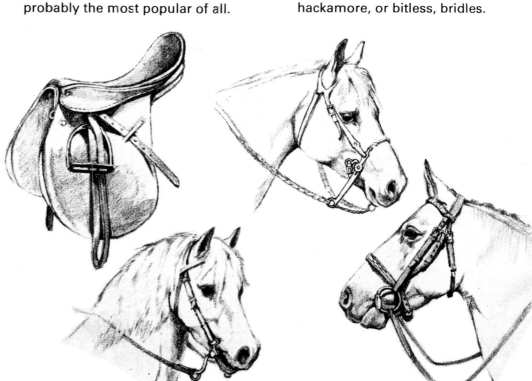

The Western saddle is often extravagantly embossed.

The fully trained Western horse is ridden in the long-cheek 'spade' bit.

The simplest form of bridle is the snaffle.

Chapter four
Riding for Fun

Enjoy riding on trekking holidays, at gymkhanas and horse shows. The more brave and skilled can compete in mounted games and other competitions. The less daring can enjoy the action from the sidelines. But really to get the best out of riding, everyone has to start at the beginning and learn the basics!

Riding should be fun, otherwise there is not much point in keeping expensive horses and ponies. But to enjoy riding, you have to learn how. The better you ride the more fun you can have. Just as we have to learn how to drive a motor-car or to play the piano, there are certain riding techniques to be learned. Riding is also complicated by the fact that it involves the comfort and welfare of another living creature, as well as ourselves.

It is possible to get the knack of sitting on a horse without falling off by going for a hack in the company of other beginners. This may be a pleasant enough occupation for some, but it has little to do with real riding. To learn to ride you must go to a school to be taught by a qualified and experienced teacher. Lessons will usually be given in an enclosed outdoor arena, or in a covered school. Here the beginner will be as safe as anyone can be when on a horse or pony. Just knowing that the horse cannot run off gives the beginner a feeling of confidence, and the presence of the instructor has the same effect.

A good school will make certain that the horse or pony is suitable for a novice rider. As far as possible, the instructor will also choose a mount that he thinks will be the most suitable for a particular pupil.

Before the beginner even gets on to the horse or pony, a good instructor will make sure that his pupil is sensibly dressed in the proper kit for the job. Nobody will mind very much about the colour of a shirt but a hard hat, properly fitting so that it will not fall off is essential. Similarly, proper boots are as essential to a horseman as climbing boots are to the mountaineer. Good boots are a sensible

A young exhibitor jumping a pony at one of the hundreds of small shows which are held every weekend in Britain during the summer season. For a pony of this size the fence is a good height.

safety measure. The substantial heel prevents the foot from slipping through the stirrup iron and the height of the boot ensures that there is no untidy gap around the ankle. Plimsolls, sandals and fashion shoes are never suitable and can be very dangerous.

Into the saddle
The pupil must first learn to mount and dismount. Mounting is usually done from the nearside, the rider holding the reins in the left hand while facing the rear and putting the left foot in the stirrup iron before swinging up and over and landing lightly as a feather in the saddle. The rider usually mounts from the near-side but, obviously, it can be very useful to have learned how to mount from the other side too.

Dismounting is accomplished by taking *both* feet out of the stirrup irons, transferring the reins to the left hand, bending the body forward and swinging the right leg over the back. The landing, on the near-side, is made on both feet and with the knees bent.

The first lessons will concentrate on the rider's position, or seat, in the saddle, for the seat is fundamental to horsemanship. Everything the rider learns subsequently depends on first having learned to sit correctly.

The position in the saddle which the instructor will be aiming for is best summed up in the words of one of the most famous riding teachers of all time, the Greek general Xenophon, who lived between 430–355 BC. Xenophon said that the seat on a horse should be that of a man standing upright, his legs apart and the knees bent. It is, indeed, as simple as that. We can, of course, add to that definition by saying that the toes point to the front, the elbows are held naturally to the sides, and the hands, thumbs on top, are held the width of the bridle's bit apart.

So far as the length of stirrup leathers is concerned, a beginner will be

Members of the Pony Club getting ready to take part in a qualifying round of the annual Prince Philip Mounted Games Championships. The Pony Club has branches all over the world.

encouraged to ride with them as long as possible without it being uncomfortable. A good length is when the base of the iron is on a level with the ankle when the leg is allowed to hang naturally.

The reason why it is good for the beginner to ride with a fairly long leather is that it encourages him to sit deeply into the lowest part of the saddle seat, rather than bouncing about on the back of the saddle because of too short a leather.

Learning with a lunge line
It is not too difficult to sit correctly while the horse or pony is standing still—the problems arise when it starts to move.

To teach the beginner to sit safely, securely and comfortably at the paces of walk, trot and canter the instructor will usually give lessons on the lunge. This means that the instructor will make the horse or pony circle round him on the end of a long line called a lunge line. The instructor controls the pony with the lunge line, his voice and by making movements with his whip to keep the pony going forward. This circling exercise is excellent for the pupil's balance and he can concentrate on his seat as he does not have to bother about controlling the pony. The pupil is allowed to hold the front of the saddle with his outside hand (i.e. the right hand if the pony is circling left and vice versa). Soon he will be made to ride without stirrups—a very good way of making the seat secure.

There are lots of suppling exercises which can be practised on the lunge. Movements like touching a toe with the fingers of the opposite hand; stretching the arms back; rotating the head and body and so on.

Good teaching schools help novices to make progress by using properly fitting saddles. These help the rider to sit centrally, which makes it much easier for the horse to carry the weight and to move in a balanced way. Later, the beginner will be taught how to 'speak' to his horse through the language of the 'natural aids'. These are the indications made by the rider with his legs and hands to convey his wishes to the horse. The legs, squeezed to the horse's sides, ask the horse to go forward. The hands receive and control that movement and act, with the legs, to make changes of direction.

Once young people, or older ones for that matter, can sit securely and control their horses with properly applied aids all sorts of activities are open to them.

Trekking holidays

Today, there are numerous riding holidays available and some of them are suitable for quite novice riders.

In Europe there are a great many trekking holidays. Usually guests stay at the place where the horses and ponies are stabled. This may be a farmhouse, and the guests look after their mounts for the duration of their holiday. Each day treks are organized from the centre and riders do not return until the evening. These treks are planned to take in the

best parts of the local countryside and often follow paths and tracks over mountains and moorland. The pace is usually fairly slow but it is a wonderful way of seeing the country.

Some centres, usually those catering for more experienced riders, organize what is called post-trekking. This means that riders set out from the centre and stay each night at a different place along the trek route. Such holidays can last a week or more and may cover long distances. One such holiday, in Spain, takes its riders through the Sierra mountains and is quite an adventure.

It is just as necessary to learn how to ride as it is to learn how to play the piano. *Top:* Most riding schools have enclosed arenas where an instructor can control a class without difficulty, and beginners can feel secure. *Above:* Trekking is now a very popular summer sport in many countries and is an ideal way to see the countryside. *Right:* Riding is not always something to be treated with deadly seriousness—it should be fun too. In this picture young riders and their ponies enjoy a fancy dress class at one of the Ponies of Britain shows.

The United States stage some wonderful riding holidays, many of them in cowboy country where guests can live in log cabins on a ranch, eat good Western food and take in the atmosphere of the Old West.

The Pony Club

For young people opportunities for riding are generally enormous, although it depends to a certain extent on where you live. If you live in Britain, or Eire, there are probably more equestrian activities than anywhere else in Europe. Young people in Britain have the advantage of being able to join the Pony Club, which is really a sort of youth club for young people interested in ponies, in looking after them and riding them. The Pony Club was founded in 1929 and it now has over 350 branches and a total of 51,000 members in Britain. The branches, which often take the name of their local hunt (e.g. the Quorn Hunt Branch of the Pony Club) cover the whole country, including the big urban and suburban areas. It would be difficult

Right and below: These young competitors are taking part in the cross-country phase of a one-day event organized by the Pony Club. The other phases are dressage and show jumping.

Right: Polo is one of the world's fastest and most exciting games. In this action picture one player is trying to 'ride-off' the other from the line of the ball, a perfectly legitimate tactic in this galloping game played by a team of four players. Polo, originally an eastern game, was brought to Europe from India by officers who had learnt the game there in the early 19th century.

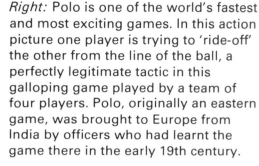

to live anywhere where there was not a Pony Club branch operating within a reasonable distance.

The Pony Club branches hold working rallies, where instruction is given in riding, stable management and so on. They also organize a winter programme of lectures, quizzes etc., and often stage a Christmas party, too. There is a full programme of area and national competitions in eventing, show jumping, dressage, pentathlon, polo and the ever-popular mounted games. All these sports culminate in national finals, and the finals of the Prince Philip Mounted Games Championship is held at the famous Horse of the Year Show at Wembley, London, each October.

Gymkhana events such as obstacle races, relays, bending races and so on are also known as mounted games. They form part of a great many of the smaller horse shows which are held in large numbers every weekend all through the summer season.

Pony Club members can also hunt at a much reduced cost. So for a young British Pony Clubber there is never a shortage of things to do with ponies.

The Pony Club is not, however, confined to Britain alone. There are no less than 1,344 branches in other countries, most particularly in the English-speaking ones, and they have a membership of some 72,000.

In continental Europe the Pony Club is still in its infancy, and there are not as yet so many opportunities for riding. The principal reason for this is the absence of any native pony breeds in the continental countries. Because there are few ponies, continental children have to learn on horses and they miss the fun of owning and looking after ponies. Continental countries have imported fairly large numbers of ponies, so they are now establishing their own pony industry.

The ideal pony

Britain is remarkably fortunate in having a wide variety of pony breeds—far more fortunate in this respect than any other country in the world. Pure-breds of these breeds or part-breds make ideal mounts for children of all ages. The smaller

The correct seat

The basis of good riding is concerned with the rider's position in the saddle. Ideally, shoulder, hip and ankle should be in one vertical line. This will ensure that the rider is sitting centrally in the saddle with the lower legs in light contact with the horse's sides. In this position the rider will be able to apply the aids without effort. Shoulders must face the front and, of course, to be in balance, the rider must not sit more to one side than to the other.

This young rider on her smartly
turned-out pony is ready to enter the
ring for one of the many pony classes
which are held at horse shows
throughout Britain during the summer
season.

native ponies include the Welsh
Mountain Pony and the slightly larger
(13 hh) Welsh Riding Pony Section B,
both of which are quality riding ponies.
The Dartmoor and the Exmoor (both
about 12 hh) are also popular mounts.
Bigger ponies (up to 14·2 hh) are the
Connemara and New Forest, both
excellent jumpers; the Dales and Fell
Ponies and the strong Highland Pony.

The Shetland is really too small for
anything but a toddler.

What is the ideal pony? In brief, it is
the one that suits the rider best and the
one that the rider suits best. A lot
depends on how the pony is to be kept;
even more depends on the ability and
temperament of the child. Finally the
cost of buying and keeping a pony has
to be taken into account. A further
consideration, which will have its effect
upon the price, is the purpose for which
the pony is required.

Obviously the pony must be the right
size for its rider. A pony may well be able
to carry the extra weight of a large rider,
but the rider will be neither comfortable

nor happy. Equally it is stupid to
'overhorse' a rider. By that we mean
buying a pony that is either too strong or
too good for its rider. There is nothing
more likely to put a beginner off riding.
Similarly, a real old Dobbin is not the
mount for a bright, brave, strong
youngster who has no nerves at all.

Price is an important factor and is
usually governed by age, appearance
and conformation, and performance. A
well-made six-year-old pony with a good
track record and a cupboard full of
rosettes will command a larger price than
a stuffy, cobby sort of 13 or 14 years
who has done nothing very much. On
the other hand, the six-year-old may

prove very expensive indeed unless the rider is good enough to do him justice, while the old pony may be just the one to give confidence to a nervous beginner. Young, inexperienced ponies, of three and four years, are not suitable for novice riders. This kind of pony needs a quiet, strong rider of some experience. Novices will do better with an older pony who knows the ropes.

Traffic-shy ponies are never a good buy. There are plenty of ponies that are safe in traffic. Unsound ponies are always expensive however cheap the purchase price as veterinary bills are never cheap. Similarly, ponies that have nasty habits, such as bucking their riders off at every opportunity should be avoided. When buying a new pony, you should always have it inspected by a veterinary surgeon to make sure it is sound and healthy. If you are in any doubt about your

Hunting is the traditional sport of the British countryside and is more popular today than ever before. This picture of the Percy Foxhounds was taken in front of the historic castle at Alnwick.

choice, it is always safer to take along an expert for a second opinion.

In general, it is more convenient, and better for the pony, if it can live out in a paddock or field the whole year round. Ponies are hardy creatures and are seldom sick or sorry. So long as they are given extra food in the winter months, when the grass has lost its goodness, they will do very well in a paddock with a decent shelter to protect them from the worst of the weather.

Riding to hounds

An exciting activity for those who can ride is the country sport of hunting. It is a sport pursued enthusiastically in Britain, Eire, the United States and Canada.

British-style hunting is concerned with the pursuit of the fox, the hare, and in some areas, the stag, by a pack of hounds. The riders follow the pack across country as well as they can within the limits imposed by farming, fencing etc. Hunting, therefore, encourages boldness and expertise in cross-country riding in both horse and rider. It is valuable experience for those aspiring to

compete in one- and three-day events.

There are as many as 300 packs of hounds in Britain and Eire and, in many instances, the numbers of followers are so large that it is necessary to ban visitors to keep the numbers or 'field' to a governable size. There are also a few packs of 'draghounds'. These are hounds that hunt an artificial scent which has been laid previously.

The ancient game of polo

Polo is a sport which was introduced to Europe by the British. They, in turn, brought the game from India in the 19th century. It is a splendid game—fast, exciting and demanding great skill. Unfortunately it is beyond the reach of many riders because of the costs involved.

Polo, however, is played extensively throughout Europe and in both North and South America. Argentine ponies (they are in fact horses but are still called ponies because there was once a height limitation of 15 hh), bred from a foundation stock of Criollo ponies crossed with Thoroughbreds, are usually considered to be the best for the game.

Chapter five
Show Jumping and Eventing

Both sports demand skill and nerve. Show jumping is now watched by millions on television, but the older and more difficult test of horse and rider is the Three-Day Event.

Show jumping has now been made universally popular by television. But it is really a very recent sport and has only achieved its great popularity within the last 30 years or so.

It is only during that time that a set of universally accepted rules has been formulated. Between the two World Wars rules were sketchy and very unsatisfactory. At one point competitions were being judged by local dignitaries on 'style' and, not surprisingly, there were some very strange results. Up to, and even after, the Second World War the fences had thin slats of wood placed along the top pole. Competitors were penalized if one of these fell off—or even if one blew off in the wind!

Pre-war courses, too, were for the most part unimaginative and often poorly built. At many agricultural shows a course would be made up of a series of upright fences, and a final water jump which was usually taken at full gallop—a sure way of ensuring that a horse got all four feet well and truly in the water.

In the early competitions time was not a factor and at smaller shows it was not unusual to see a competitor turn away from a fence because he was not quite 'on the right stride'. He would then repeat his approach and try again.

Although the rules were vague it should not be thought that the standards were correspondingly low. In international jumping the standards were high. The pre-war years produced

horsemen of the calibre of Colonel Rodzianko, Colonel Joe Hume-Dudgeon Commandants Aherne and Corry of Ireland, and Colonel Sir Michael Ansell, the creator of the great London international shows, who is often called the father of modern show jumping. Pre-war jumping also featured the high jump, a competition which is not so popular now and indeed, is only rarely seen.

Show jumping today

Modern show jumping is far more developed and vastly more sophisticated. Unlike the jumping of fifty years ago, which took place only during the summer months, it continues throughout the year in indoor and outdoor arenas all over the world.

The name 'show' jumping was given to the sport because most of the competitions took place as part of conventional agricultural and horse shows. It also pointed out the difference between jumping across country, or

Hunter trials are first cousins to the sport of eventing and are often used as an introduction to it. These two riders are competing in a 'pairs' class, a competition usually included in hunter trials.

when out hunting, and the jumping of coloured fences within a show ring. In Britain, however, jumping competitions were also frequently referred to in show catalogues as 'Horse Leaping'.

There are variations in national rules but for the most part, show jumping rules throughout the world conform to the agreed pattern operated by national bodies and agreed by the International Federation.

There are six distinct types of competition, which are generally recognized. There is first the type in which competitors who are still equal after two jump-offs over raised fences divide the prize money; secondly, the type in which time counts in the second jump-off and the fastest time with the least number of faults is the winner;

Left: Eventing is one of the toughest of horse sports, demanding the utmost of horse and rider. Most cross-country courses involve water obstacles like this one which American team member Bruce Davidson tackles during the Munich Olympics. *Right:* Eddie Macken, the great stylist of the Irish show jumping team, rides Kerrygold over one of the big fences at Hickstead's All-England Jumping Arena.

A brilliant American combination, Mary Chapot and White Lightning, competing at the Hickstead Arena, Sussex. This is a permanent jumping course holding meetings throughout the season.

thirdly comes the competition in which the clock is used in the same way in the first jump-off; the fourth type is purely a speed competition, the round with the least number of jumping faults in the

fastest time winning the competition.

There are then timed competitions, which might be called 'novelty jumping'. These include Take Your Own Line, Scurry and Pair Relays, in which, instead of faults for knockdowns etc., 6–10 seconds are added to the total time taken for each fence which is knocked down.

Finally, there are those Hit and Hurry, Accumulator and Have a Gamble competitions. In these competitions fences are considered to be worth a certain number of points if jumped without a knockdown. These competitions have their own special rules. Fences in speed competitions are always lower than in the others so that horses are not over-taxed.

The basic rules of jumping, apart from those competitions in which time faults are given, are: four faults for a knockdown, three for a first refusal, six for a second and elimination for a third. The fall of horse and rider, or of the rider alone, is penalized with eight faults.

Building the course

Modern show jumping courses, with their brightly coloured fences decorated with banks of flowers and rows of shrubs, appear to be very elaborate and to include a large variety of obstacles. But all the fences in the arena fall into one of three categories: uprights, parallels and spreads. This is the basic theme, the variations being represented by walls, stiles, oxers and crossed poles.

In the big, outdoor arenas, like those at Hamburg, Hickstead and Arena North, natural obstacles are also included. The most notable ones are those which involve jumping from one level to another, water jumps, or fences incorporating water, and big, awesome banks.

All fences, depending on their height, shape and width, present specific problems within themselves, but the bigger problems are caused by the layout of the course and the distances between the fences.

Fences which are placed less than 39 ft 4 in (11·98 m) apart are called combination fences and are numbered as being one fence. The easy distance between fences in combination is about 24 ft (7·3 m). This allows a horse to land over the first element and then to take one stride before taking off over the second. A distance of 33 ft (10 m),

Right: James Day is one of the very talented members of the Canadian team. Here he is pictured on Simpatico clearing a very big spread of parallel rails in fine style.

Fences

Show jumping fences are built so that the coloured poles fall when hit. Those used in cross-country courses at horse trials are fixed and rustic in appearance. Some show jumping arenas, such as Hickstead in England, do, however, include fixed, cross-country type fences in their courses. It is not only the size of the fences that counts. Sharp twists and turns make the course more difficult.

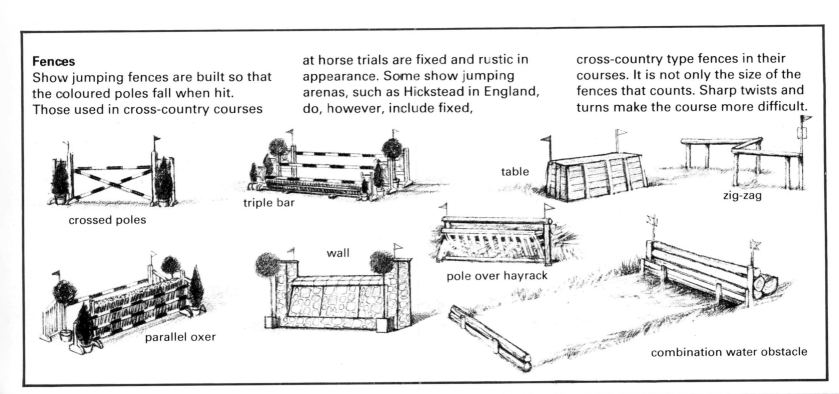

crossed poles

triple bar

table

zig-zag

parallel oxer

wall

pole over hayrack

combination water obstacle

allows for two non-jumping strides.

In novice competitions these distances will be kept to very strictly. In advanced classes the distances may be shortened or lengthened a little so that the horse has to take a half-stride. This shortening or lengthening of the stride so as to arrive correctly at the take-off point is difficult and requires an expert rider and a very supple and obedient horse.

Distances between fences are very important and have to be measured carefully by the course-builder. Allowance has to be made in the distance according to the type of fence employed in combination. In the case of a parallel followed by an upright the distance has to be increased, otherwise after spreading over the first fence there would be no room for the horse to take off over the second. If it was the other way round, an upright and then a parallel, the distance has to be made shorter if the horse is going to be able to stretch over the spread of the second part of the combination.

Big jumping events are held each year at shows in London, Hamburg, Aachen, Paris, Rome, New York, Toronto and elsewhere. There are also the great events: the Olympic Games held every four years, the World Championships held every four years and the European Championships held every two years. In addition, both Hickstead, in England, and Hamburg in Germany hold 'Derby' meetings.

Famous favourites

Because of television, show jumping stars are as well known as soccer heroes in Europe or baseball stars in America. Everyone knows of David Broome, a champion many times over, and of Harvey Smith, who is always a favourite, even if today he tends to take a back seat in favour of his son Robert. Caroline Bradley and Liz Edgar, David Broome's sister, are firm favourites everywhere they go. Ireland's Eddie Macken is the heart throb of the teenager, and the dashing, if diminutive, Paul Darragh has

audiences bouncing in their seats with excitement. The same goes for the most forceful rider of them all, Austria's Hugo Simon who rides his big horses, like Gladstone and Lavendel, with enormous vigour. Gerd Wiltfang, the World Champion from Germany, is a much more relaxed character—until the chips are down and he is riding for life and his titles on horses like Roman or the huge grey Askan. Other members of the German squad, as well known abroad as in their own country, are Fritz Ligges and Paul Schockemöhle. His brother Alwin Schockemöhle, has now retired from active riding because of a back injury and is making a name for himself as a course builder.

The Americans are the stylists of today. They sit in the classical riding position demanded by their gifted Hungarian-born trainer, Bert de Nemethy. Six of their leading riders are William (Buddy) Brown, Rodney Jenkins, Michael Matz, George Morris, Katie Monahan and Melanie Smith, all of

Left: Marion Mould and her remarkable pony Stroller, on whom she won nearly every major jumping award as well as an Olympic silver medal. *Above:* Richard Meade, the veteran British Three-day Event rider and winner of two Olympic gold medals, rides Jacob Jones confidently into the Lake at the Badminton Horse Trials. This event is held every spring on the Duke of Beaufort's Badminton estate. *Below:* The Badminton Lake obstacle claims another victim. The Lake is always one of the principal hazards at these famous Trials and has always been a part of the cross-country course.

whom have competed successfully in Europe, and there are plenty more.

But the best loved of them all are probably the remarkable d'Inzeo brothers, Raimondo and Piero. These two Italian riders have been at the top of international show jumping for some 30 years or more and can still show the way to the youngsters.

Eventing

The sport of eventing, or Horse Trials, is a very different and less artificial one. It is, incidentally, the sport in which Britain's Princess Anne competes so successfully. Her Highness is not, as the newspapers would have us believe, 'a show jumper'. On the other hand the Princess was the European Individual Three-Day Event Champion in 1971, riding Doublet, a horse owned by HM The Queen. In 1974 Princess Anne was a member of the British team that won a silver medal in the World Championships and she was a member of the British Olympic team at Montreal.

Modern horse trials developed from a much earlier army sport, known appropriately as The Military. This was a test designed to prove the fitness of man and horse on active service. The test was based on the idea of a mounted man carrying military despatches across country, surmounting obstacles and hazards as they were encountered. In

time the test developed to include a dressage test to show the horse's obedience and suppleness, and a final arena jumping phase on the day following the cross-country to prove that horse and rider were still fit for service. The modern test is similarly based but has been still further extended.

As an introduction to the full-blooded, top-level three-day horse trials, there are numerous one- and two-day events organized for novice and intermediate standard horses. The basic phases of

Champion of Champions—Lucinda Prior-Palmer, a former World and European Three-day Event Champion, four times winner of the Badminton Horse Trials and a member of the British Olympic team, on Be Fair.

dressage, cross-country and arena jumping are still included, although each test is scaled down to suit the standard of the novice or intermediate horses.

The dressage test
The opening phase of the three-day horse trial is the dressage test and it is just as difficult to perform successfully as any of the tests in the other phases. A really fit horse, ready to gallop for his life over steeplechase and cross-country fences, is asked to perform a relatively complex test and to do so calmly and obediently. This is a great test of horsemanship and training.

Dressage is a French word which means training or schooling, and the object of the dressage test in the three-day event is to prove that the

horse's training has made him obedient, supple, balanced and gymnastic. The test should be performed with fluid grace, active, accurate and graceful in the transitions from one pace or movement to another, and without any signs of resistance on the part of the horse. Above all, the event horse must always be 'going forward'. He must never appear to be hanging back or unwilling to go into contact with his rider's hands.

Dressage is an Olympic discipline in itself, like the three-day event or show jumping. However, in this context, dressage should not be confused with the Horse Trials dressage test. The Olympic test is much more advanced, and includes the classical *pirouettes*, *passage* and *piaffe* movements which are

Sheila Willcox, formerly an event rider, took up dressage after she had a serious accident at the Wylye Trials. Here she is seen competing on Sun and Air at the Goodwood Dressage Championships.

not required in the event horse.

The Horse Trials dressage test is carried out in an arena measuring 198 ft×66 ft (60 m×20 m) and is ridden before three judges. Scoring is by a system of penalties, the lowest score winning. This is the opposite to the pure dressage competition, in which the highest number of marks heads the final placings.

The Speed and Endurance Test

In Horse Trials, it is the second day's Speed and Endurance Test, at the centre of which is the cross-country phase, which is the most critical part of the event. This test has four phases. Phases A and C consist of Roads and Tracks which may be between 6–12 miles (9-19 km) in overall length. This distance has to be covered at a stipulated speed which involves trotting for most of the way with occasional stretches at canter. In between phases A and C is the steeplechase course, Phase B. This is usually over twelve 'chasing fences. This must be ridden at a good gallop if competitors are not to be penalized for exceeding the time limit.

The fourth phase is undertaken after a ten minute break following Phase C. It is the cross-country course. This is between 3–5 miles (5–8 km) long, over 30–40 big and imposing obstacles sited to make the best use of the natural ground hazards. Considerable use is made of water—at the Badminton Horse Trials in Great Britain the Lake fences are well known, as is the famous Trout Hatchery at Burghley. There are also usually some formidable drop fences, and combinations such as 'farmyards', 'quarries', and the notorious 'coffin' obstacles. Many fences are built to allow alternative ways of jumping them. The short way, which saves time, is for the brave and bold, the longer way for the more circumspect on the tired horse.

Riders are given 20 penalties for a first refusal at a fence, 40 for a second at the same fence and are eliminated for a third refusal at the same obstacle. Falls cost a rider 60 penalties and three falls on the course means elimination. There are also penalties for exceeding the time limit in any one phase.

On the final day the jumping test takes place, following a veterinary examination. The course is not particularly difficult but after the exertions of the previous day it is none the less a stiff test of fitness and courage.

Fences knocked down in this phase cost five penalties and a first refusal three; the second refusal is penalized six and the third earns elimination.

The principal three-day events are those held at Badminton and Burghley, England; Boekelo in Holland, Luhmuhlen in Germany; Punchestown, Ireland, and Ledyard Farm, in the United States.

Without doubt the three-day event is the most severe test of horse and rider of all the equestrian disciplines.

Chapter six
The Show Ring

The show ring calls for showmanship. Manes are plaited, hooves oiled and coats groomed until they gleam. Well-polished show tack is the order of the day. In short, every effort is made to present to the judge a horse or pony looking as near to perfection as possible.

Horse shows, or horse fairs, have been a feature of country life for centuries. To a very large degree their main purpose has not changed, even though today this purpose is not always appreciated.

The horse show provides an opportunity for people to see how their horses and ponies compare with others. It also serves as a sort of 'shop window' for breeders and professional showmen. But there is an underlying purpose more important than either of those. Horse shows play an important part in improving breeds and types of horses and ponies, as well as encouraging higher standards of presentation. In a way, many of the show classes are 'beauty competitions' and the horses that win set an example which will be followed by other breeders and exhibitors. Whether show classes are for horses and ponies shown 'in-hand' (the American term is 'halter' class) or under saddle, they are held to decide which type of animal is considered best for a particular job. The judges are looking for the near-perfect specimen. How the judges make their decision and the kinds of classes which are held vary from one country to another.

In Britain, where more horse shows are held in the summer months than in any other country in the world, there are a huge number of classes for ridden horses and ponies, for harness animals, and for exhibits shown in-hand in the breed classes. With local variations the same kinds of classes are found at the big shows in South Africa, such as the annual Rand Show, and in Australia at shows such as the enormous one held in Sydney. In continental Europe, horse shows operate rather differently. They

A charming picture of a young competitor showing her pony in a side-saddle. There has been a revival of side-saddle riding in recent years owing to the formation of associations that actively support it.

have no hunters, which form the bulk of the British show classes, and except at specific breed shows, there would be insufficient entries for pony breeding classes—much less for ridden ponies.

The big Continental shows, however, stage many exciting driving classes and, as well as the show jumping (the crowd-pulling feature for most shows), they also stage high-level dressage competitions. Some of the bigger British shows also stage dressage competitions, but they are usually in rings far away from the main arena, and cannot be considered as 'show' classes.

American horse shows are probably the most diverse in the world and the really big ones have hunter and pony classes (judged differently from British ones), driving classes, classes for special breeds and lots of Western classes.

Judging show classes

With shows following the British pattern the in-hand classes include stallions, brood mares and youngstock (from foals and yearlings up to three-year-olds). These are also divided by breed or type. At a big show like the Royal Windsor Horse Show, there may be classes for hunters in-hand, for the Mountain and Moorland breeds (the native ponies), for Arabs and perhaps even for Appaloosas and Palominos.

In these classes the judge or judges (there will never be more than two) assess the conformation of the animals before them, bearing in mind the purpose for which they are used. 'Conformation' is the word used for the make and shape of the horse. It is concerned with the strength of the frame, with the shape of the individual parts making up the whole and with the proper proportion of one part to another. Once the animals have been lined up in a preliminary order, the judges examine each animal individually. They have it walked and trotted out so that they can see how good, or

This is a pairs class at one of the big Australian shows. The ponies, unlike those in show classes elsewhere in the world, carry their numbers around their necks, but the show is still the thing!

otherwise, is the animal's action.

The turnout of horses and ponies in in-hand classes varies according to the class. Hunters, for instance, are always shown with the mane plaited and with the tail either pulled (shaped by pulling out hairs at the dock) and 'banged' (cutting the tail square in line with the point of the hocks), or the top third may be plaited. Native ponies are not shown plaited, although occasionally New Forests are the exception to this unwritten ruling. Palominos, too, are shown unplaited, and under no circumstance is the mane and tail of an Arab pulled, plaited or interfered with in any other way. All in-hand animals have their feet oiled before entering the ring and most exhibitors rub a little grease round the eyes and nostrils and under the dock to give a little extra refinement. All these cosmetic touches are a matter of showmanship and are aimed at catching the eye of the judge. They are all quite legitimate, but they are not compulsory.

British ridden hunter classes are of two sorts. There are the 'show' hunters in the three weight categories—heavy, middle and lightweight—ladies hunters (ridden sidesaddle), and 'small' hunters under 15·2 hh. These classes are judged on the action at walk, trot, canter and, most importantly, at gallop; on conformation and on the ride (for the judge or judges ride the exhibits for themselves).

The horses do not have to jump. The theory is that if a horse is of near-perfect proportions, is sound and able to move well at all paces, then he should be able to carry a man across country quickly and safely without strain to himself. Jumping in the ring under unnatural conditions with such horses proves

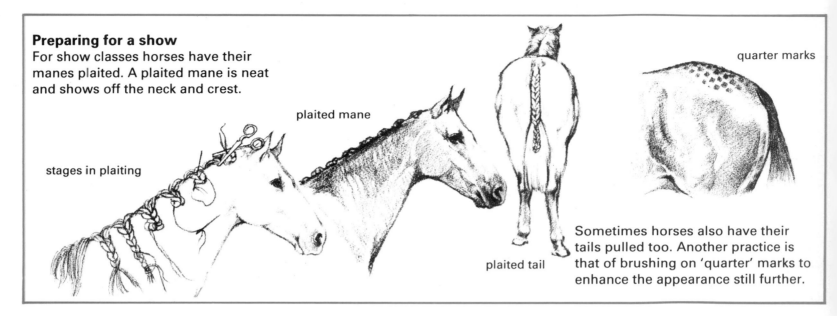

Preparing for a show
For show classes horses have their manes plaited. A plaited mane is neat and shows off the neck and crest.

stages in plaiting

plaited mane

plaited tail

quarter marks

Sometimes horses also have their tails pulled too. Another practice is that of brushing on 'quarter' marks to enhance the appearance still further.

The lovely head of a Welsh Cob, one of the most spectacular of the British native breeds. The Welsh Cob is famous for its unique trotting action. It is a larger edition of the Welsh Mountain Pony and may stand as much as 15 hh.

nothing which is relevant to the matter in hand. It is taken for granted that a horse with the right physical characteristics will be able to jump, or be taught to do so.

There are, however, classes for 'working' hunters, in which the exhibits have to jump a course of rustic fences. The judging in these classes is, in consequence, strongly biased towards performance and the odd bump or blemish, honourably gained on the hunting field, is not held against an exhibit.

Hunters under saddle in show classes are always plaited up and, although there is no ruling about it, are expected to be shown in double bridles. Working hunters are, however, permitted to wear snaffles, drop nosebands and even a martingale, but they too are always plaited.

Hack classes are held at most shows. Hacks are riding horses and are usually Thoroughbreds. Long ago there were two sorts, a covert hack and a park hack. The covert hack was the heavier of the two and was used to carry his master to the meet of the hunt at a sharp canter. Once there the rider changed to his hunter and the hack was taken home. The park hack was lighter, more elegant, very well-mannered and schooled and with exceptionally smooth paces. Its purpose was to cut a dash for its rider before the admiring pedestrians in the park. It is the park hack that is shown today. In hack classes riders have to give an individual show, although the judge also rides the entries himself.

Ponies have three height classes, up to 12·2 hh, up to 13·2 hh and up to 14·2

hh. They also give individual displays but, of course, are not ridden by the judges. In show catalogues ridden ponies are described as 'children's ponies' and they are judged on their suitability as high-quality, all-round ponies for child riders. Particular note, therefore, is taken of their behaviour in the ring. Like the show hunters, show ponies do not jump in the ring, but there are 'working' hunter pony classes, on the same lines as those for working hunters, which give a chance to the more ordinary sort of pony who would not do well in a 'beauty competition'. Show ponies are, for the most part, also shown in double bridles.

Showmanship

All entries in horse show classes are groomed until they shine. Very often the grooming extends to 'quarter marks', patterns brushed in the hair on the top of the quarters. Nothing is too much trouble and great attention is paid to saddlery and turnout. In ridden classes, certainly in the pure show classes, competitors use a saddle which is nearly cut straight downwards in front. This is not at all like the jumping saddles where the flaps are cut well forward. The object of these show-type saddles is to show off the horse's 'front', by which is meant the slope of the shoulder and the 'length of rein'—the distance along the top side of the neck. A straight saddle does not, obviously, cover up the shoulder as much as one which has forward-cut

Above right: The final line-up in a pony show class with the winners wearing their rosettes. These are novice ponies and snaffle bridles are encouraged rather than the usual double bridle.
Right: A young competitor determined that the judges should see her pony to best advantage. The art of showing a pony in-hand is just as skilful as showing a pony under saddle.

flaps. If the horse does not have a very good front, competitors hope that by using a straight-cut show saddle, pushed well back, the judge will be fooled into thinking that the front is better than it actually is—he won't, but it's legitimate showmanship.

At some shows there are classes for cobs, a peculiarly English institution. Cobs are animals with great character. They have big bodies carried on four short, stout legs. Their purpose is to provide an enjoyable ride for older, heavier riders who want a steady performance with no fireworks. Cobs are, none the less, judged as hunters, but Cobs always appear with 'hogged' manes—the American term is 'roach' manes. This means that the mane has been given a crew cut with a pair of clippers.

American ridden classes differ in that they are judged almost entirely on performance, style and turnout. This is the case in Western classes, too. In addition, American judges, and there can be a number judging a class, never touch the exhibits, let alone ride them. Recently, American classes have been judged rather like skating competitions, each judge giving a mark which is immediately flashed onto a board.

In Europe the 'Swedish system' is also practised in assessing in-hand classes. In this system each member of a panel of judges marks the horses part by part: so much for head and neck, so much for shoulders etc., the marks are then averaged. This system, however, involves the employment of a number of judges. It is not always practical when there are many horse shows taking place simultaneously, so that the limited number of judges available would be insufficient to provide the members necessary for a panel.

Harness horses

Driving classes form an increasingly large part of shows in Europe and the United States. British classes include the very

Top left: The glamour of the show ring. This picture is of the judging during the annual Thoroughbred Stallion Show held by the Hunters' Improvement Society each year at Tattersall's Park Paddocks, Newmarket, the headquarters of British racing. *Left:* The coaching class of four-in-hands leaves the ring after being judged at Britain's Royal Agricultural Society of England Show. Coaching classes, usually preceded by a marathon drive, are a feature at most major shows. *Right:* A prize-winning Shire stallion, his showing bridle decorated with the winner's rosette.

specialized Hackney turnouts for single and pair harness as well as numerous 'private' turnout classes. The Hackney is, perhaps, the supreme harness horse, being a spectacular high-stepper with great fire and dash. However, the Hackney's usefulness is confined to the show ring, whereas the more ordinary pony, cob or horse exhibited in the 'private' classes can be driven pleasurably on the roads.

In these last classes, as in the case of coaching classes, judging is often

preceded by a 'marathon' drive finishing in the show ring. In these classes great attention is paid to the correctness of turnout and the suitability of the horse and the vehicle.

In the United States the harness classes are dominated largely by Hackneys and by the American Saddler, which is also a driving horse. However, there are also classes for the versatile Morgan horse and for the American Shetland, a pony that resembles a Hackney very closely.

Chapter seven
Racing – the sport of kings

Whether racing on the flat, steeplechasing or trotting, there is nothing more exciting than the battle for first place as horse and rider put everything they've got into the final furlong.

The oldest established form of modern racing, and the most important, is racing on the flat. This is known as 'the sport of kings'. It got that name because of the interest taken in racehorse breeding and racing by successive British monarchs.

Royal studs were kept by the Tudors and early Stuarts and both James I and Charles I raced horses at the little town of Newmarket in Suffolk. With the Restoration in 1660 came Charles II, a king passionately addicted to the sport. It was he who organized racing at Newmarket, established a set of rules and frequently acted as arbiter in disputes. Successive monarchs gave their support to racing. Queen Anne, for instance, was responsible for racing being started at Ascot and today HM Queen Elizabeth is a very knowledgeable patron of the turf. She is closely involved in the breeding and racing of Thoroughbred horses.

It was, however, the establishment of the Thoroughbred as a breed in its own right that laid the foundations for modern racing all over the world.

The Arabian sires

The Thoroughbred was developed in England from three Arabian sires. All the world's Thoroughbreds are descended from these three horses. The Byerley Turk was responsible for the Herod line through his great-great grandson King Herod. Herod was a successful racehorse in his own right but he was just as good as a stallion, siring the winners of 1,042 races worth £200,000. Herod also sired Highflyer, another very successful horse whose progeny won 1,108 races valued at £170,000. Highflyer made a fortune for his owner Richard Tattersall. This was the Tattersall

Tension at the start as the jockeys wait in the starting stalls for the 'off'. Starting stalls are used for all flat races but for steeplechasing a simple starting tape is still in use.

who founded the world-famous British firm of bloodstock auctioneers, which still operates the prestigious sales held at Newmarket. Buyers flock to these sales from all over the world.

The second of the Eastern sires was the Darley Arabian, imported in 1704. He was the sire of the first great racehorse, Flying Childers, and the great-great grandsire of what was perhaps the greatest racehorse of all time, the legendary Eclipse. Eclipse's somewhat disreputable owner Dennis O'Kelly coined the phrase, 'Eclipse first, the rest nowhere'. Eclipse, who was never extended, let alone beaten, raced over long distances up to four miles (6·4 km), and carried weights as much as 12 st (76 kg). He laid the foundations of courage and staying power in the Thoroughbred, and founded a dynasty. Among his descendants was St Simon, winner of the 1884 Gold Cup at Ascot and the greatest racehorse of his day. He headed the winning sire's list nine times,

Top: Racehorses at exercise. In Britain and Ireland horses are trained at stables sited usually around the main racing centres, and are exercised and galloped on heath or downland. In America horses are stabled and trained on the racetracks. *Above:* This action picture has caught the horses just as they have left the stalls.

a feat never achieved before or since. From St Simon descends the Italian horse Ribot, unbeaten in his career.

Seventy-four per cent of the winners of the Derby have been descendants of Eclipse. Of the 15 winners of the Triple Crown, which is three races together, the 2,000 Guineas, the Derby and the St Leger, all but one descend from Eclipse.

The third member of the trio of founding fathers was the Godolphin Arabian. He was the grandsire of Matchem who, like Herod and Eclipse, founded an outstanding male line to which America's fabulous Man O'War

Horse and jockey

The art of race-riding is very skilful. The jockey must always be able to keep his horse balanced even when his mount is tired and has to be ridden hard in a finish. The coloured blouses and caps worn by jockeys are called silks and are made in the horse owner's colours.

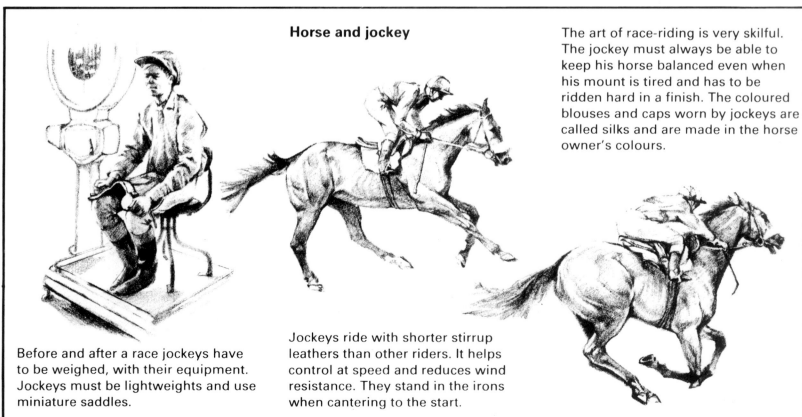

Before and after a race jockeys have to be weighed, with their equipment. Jockeys must be lightweights and use miniature saddles.

Jockeys ride with shorter stirrup leathers than other riders. It helps control at speed and reduces wind resistance. They stand in the irons when cantering to the start.

Left: Specially shod horses race regularly at the winter meetings held at St Moritz, Switzerland. *Above:* The real winter sport, however, is steeplechasing and this exciting picture of the field taking the open ditch at Navan, Eire, typifies the spirit of the 'jumping game'. *Right:* Just as popular as ridden races in America, Australia and many European countries is the sport of trotting.

belonged. Known to millions of Americans as 'Big Red' he was as well known to racegoers of the 1920s as the great, and very valuable, Secretariat is to modern-day racing enthusiasts.

The Jockey Club, the governing body of racing and the model for all other racing countries, was founded in Newmarket in about 1750. Today its authority is absolute in British racing.

As time passed horses were raced at younger ages and over shorter distances. The English 'classic' races were designed to encourage the production of a three-year-old capable of racing over one mile (1,600 m) in the spring and reaching one and three quarter miles (2,800 m) in the autumn. The first of the 'classics' is the one-mile 2,000 Guineas for colts, first run in 1809. The equivalent for fillies is the 1,000 Guineas (1819). They are both run at Newmarket. The one and a half mile (2,400 m) races run at Epsom are the Derby (1780) and Oaks (for fillies, first held in 1779). Finally there is the St Leger (1778) run over one and three quarter miles (2,800 m) at Doncaster in September.

Racing in the USA

Racing in the States started with the

early colonists who founded the Quarter Horse breed to race over 440 yd (402 m) tracks cut out of the forests.

Thoroughbreds, however, were soon being imported from England. Among them was the winner of the first Derby, Sir Charles Bunbury's Diomed. Though this horse was a failure as a sire in England, it produced good stock in America.

The greatest American stallion of the 19th century was Lexington, champion sire on no less than 16 occasions.

The American classic three-year-old races were all established in the decade following the Civil War. They are the Belmont Stakes, now run at New York's Belmont Park (1½ miles—2,400 m), the Preakness Stakes held at Baltimore (1 mile 1½ furlongs—1,900 m) and the Kentucky Derby run at Churchill Downs, Louisville.

An early American-bred horse to win the English Derby was Iroquois in 1891. More recently there has been Sir Ivor (1968), Mill Reef (1971) and Roberto in 1972. Nijinsky, the winner in 1970 was bred in Canada.

America is now the leading racing nation with prize money reaching an annual total approaching $175 million. Some 26,000 Thoroughbred foals are bred each year in the United States. This is three times as many as are bred in Britain and six times the number bred in France, the other major influence in Thoroughbred racing.

In terms of numbers, Australia and New Zealand rank second to North America. There are some 25,000 horses competing for a $25 million prize money each year. The breeding industry is strong, although 50 per cent of the top 500 sires are imported horses.

The great centres of Thoroughbred breeding in England and America are, in the first instance, around the headquarters of racing at Newmarket. A lesser number of studs also operate in the Lambourn area and in Yorkshire. The most important area in the States is the Blue Grass of Kentucky, where horse-breeding is the major industry.

Steeplechasing favourites

Steeplechasing involves racing over jumps and is carried on in most racing countries. Nowhere is it so developed and so popular as in Britain and Ireland. As it does not support a major breeding industry it cannot achieve the importance of flat racing, nor, of course, is it so old a sport. It has its roots in the hunting field although the first steeplechase is said to have been the one between Cornelius O'Callaghan and Edmund Blake. In 1752 they rode their

Above: A portrait of one of the world's greatest horses, the mighty Arkle. His greatest victories were at Cheltenham where he was the winner of three Cheltenham Gold Cups. *Left:* A steeplechase jockey takes the precaution of knotting his reins before leaving the paddock.

hunters from Buttevant Church to St Leger Steeple in Co. Cork, Ireland. But steeplechasing did not become firmly established until the 19th century. The first jumping meeting was held in 1830, and was arranged at St Albans by Tom Colman, proprietor of the Turf Hotel. Perhaps the best known steeplechase is the Grand National. The first one was held at Aintree, Liverpool, in 1839 and was won by Lottery ridden by a professional jockey, Jem Mason.

None the less, steeplechasing seems to produce the greatest and best-loved equine characters.

There was the wonder horse of the thirties, Golden Miller, who held the course record for the Grand National until 1973 when Red Rum completed the course in a shade over nine minutes. Golden Miller's forte, however, was not the Aintree course. He made this quite clear in his subsequent performances there. His course was Cheltenham and his race was the Gold Cup which he won every year between 1932 and 1936. His greatest triumph was to win both the National and the Gold Cup in one year, 1934; a feat never achieved before or since.

More recently, there was the great Arkle, a personality if ever there was one and, of course, Red Rum himself.

Perhaps Arkle's most memorable races were in 1964. This was his best season, when he beat his only serious rival the big English horse, Mill House, for he was victorious in the Hennessy at Newbury after having beaten Mill House in one of the greatest Cheltenham Gold Cups ever seen. Owned by Anne, Duchess of Westminster, and trained by Tom Dreaper in Ireland, Arkle was always ridden by jockey Pat Taaffe who had a particular way with him.

Red Rum is an out-and-out Aintree specialist. Though retired, this remarkable horse is now a pop star and makes personal appearances throughout Britain. He has the all-time record of three Grand National wins, in 1973, '74 and '77, and two second places in the same race in 1975 and '76.

Trotting

The amateur counterpart of steeplechasing, or National Hunt racing, is the hunt point-to-points which are held in large numbers between February and early May. There is, however, another form of racing, little known in Britain but enormously popular on the Continent, in the United States and in Australia and New Zealand. This is the sport of trotting, which is largely dominated by the American Standardbred pacer. One Standardbred of the 1930s who did much to popularize trotting in America was a horse called Greyhound, whose world trotting record of 1 minute 55¾ seconds for the mile (1,600 m) remained unbeaten for thirty-one years.

Another famous horse was the New Zealand-bred Cardigan Bay, a pacer who raced at home and in the States. This horse frequently paced the mile in under two minutes and was the first to break the million-dollar barrier in stakes money.

Horses like these encouraged the sport and in 1940 New York's Roosevelt Raceway introduced night racing, which is now a feature of the sport. It was also the Roosevelt Raceway which, in 1946, introduced the mobile starting gate. This is attached to a motor vehicle driven ahead of the horses and ensures an even start.

A raceway is usually an oval track of half a mile (800 m) and is wide enough to take eight horses abreast. The average distance of races is one mile (1,600 m).

The French have a big trotting industry which claims a greater following than flat-racing. They have developed their own trotting breed, the French Trotter. The bigger horses race at the trot under saddle!

Two of the greatest racehorses in the world, both Derby winners.
Below: Nijinsky, the Canadian-bred horse who won the Derby in 1970.
Bottom: The American-bred Mill Reef, who won the Derby in 1971.

Chapter eight
Looking after Horses

It is natural for a horse or pony to live out in a field or paddock, but it still needs constant care. Looking after a stabled horse is even more demanding but a happy, healthy horse is worth the effort.

There are three methods of horse-keeping in general use. The horse can be housed in a stable; or it can live out in a paddock; or it can be kept on what is sometimes called the combined system. This last method, as the name suggests, combines the use of the field and the stable. The horse is kept stabled for most of the time but is allowed to run out in the paddock for some hours during the day. If it is winter and the horse has been clipped, a waterproof New Zealand rug is put on to keep it from catching cold.

It is possible to keep horses, and more particularly ponies, at grass throughout the year, but this method limits the use which can be made of the animal and is not suitable for all horses.

Thoroughbreds and pure-bred Arabian horses, or animals which are closely related to either, will rarely do well if kept out at grass the whole year round. The more common animals and the cobby sorts are more able to manage at grass and ponies are often better for being kept out, usually remaining very healthy.

Nonetheless, although it is more natural for a horse to live out, it should not be thought that it will be able to maintain good condition, much less do any work, on grass alone. As the winter approaches the growth stops and during the winter months there is little nutrient value in grass. It is, therefore, necessary to feed grass-kept animals extra rations of hay, and probably horse cubes or nuts as well, during the winter. In the summer months, when the grass is growing and is at its best, horses and ponies will do very well on what they get from their paddock—so long as the paddock is big enough and offers grass in quantity and

The farrier putting the final touches to a new set of shoes. Shoeing is necessary to prevent the feet becoming sore when the horse is ridden on roads and rough surfaces. It is a highly skilled job.

quality. As a general rule 1½ acres (0·6 hectares) per head is considered to be the minimum requirement and 2–3 acres (0·8–1·2 hectares) would not be too much.

Grass, however, is a soft food and although it will keep horses and ponies in good condition during the summer it does not provide the extra energy they need for work. For that reason horses and ponies which are required to work during the summer are best brought into a stable for part of the day. This helps to preserve their figures and prevents them from becoming overweight. During the summer, one of the problems facing the owner of grass-kept horses is overweight in their animals. This is particularly so with ponies, who by their nature are more efficient converters of food. In the first place, too much weight restricts the use of the animal. A fat horse cannot be expected to work effectively. Secondly, too much grass can give rise to the distressing foot complaint called laminitis, which is a 'fever' of the feet—the feet become gorged with blood, highly inflamed and very painful. Horses which are brought into the stable can be fed 'short' feeds of concentrates such as oats, nuts and bran.

Field management
In the wild state, the problems of horse-sick pastures and red-worm infestation do not arise because of the vast areas over which the wild horses can graze. In the domestic state, however, where horses are confined to small areas, pastures can quickly become horse-sick. The horse is a wasteful grazer, choosing only the tastiest morsels and avoiding rank grasses which spring up where droppings have lain. There is, therefore, a grass-management problem. Droppings should be removed, the land should be regularly fertilized and, if possible, should be grazed in rotation with other land.

Worm-control is even more important.

A girl harness-maker at work. Previously a trade confined almost entirely to men, an increasing number of saddlers and harness-makers today are women.

All horses carry a certain number of worms inside them. Worms can be controlled by regular dosing with a proprietary wormer. In small paddocks, however, worm control is made more difficult because the worm eggs pass out with the droppings, hatch in the grass and then re-enter the horse's body with every mouthful of grass that is eaten.

Even where plenty of land is available, there are still conditions to be met by the horse-owner. Paddocks need a good supply of clean water, which is easily accessible. Water is best supplied by a field pipe to a trough which can be emptied for cleaning and has no sharp edges. Stagnant water in ponds etc. is not suitable. There must be shelter from prevailing winds, which can be hedges or a clump of trees, or a shelter. There must be adequate, safe fencing and the field itself must be free from anything likely to cause injury. Finally, horses and ponies at grass need regular and constant supervision.

Horses and ponies out at grass in winter, sometimes do not use their field shelter. So long as they are being adequately fed, they may prefer to stand under hedges or trees, where these exist. In winter, horses grow thick coats as a protection against the cold and wet. They also develop a film of waterproofing grease on the skin to give protection against rain and snow. Horses at grass in the winter must not, therefore, be groomed which would remove the protective grease from the coat. Nor should the coat be removed by clipping unless a New Zealand rug is fitted, a good shelter provided and the horse fed generous quantities of food.

In all cases, where natural shelter is not available, a field shelter should be provided to protect the animals from the

Horses love to roll! Apart from the obvious pleasure experienced, horses will roll to clean themselves if they have been sweating and also to get rid of skin irritations.

cold winds. It should be sited out of the prevailing wind. In summer a shelter will provide shade and the horses will use it to escape flies and other insects.

Safe fencing is best provided by a good thick hedge, but where boundary hedges are thin or non-existent artificial fencing has to be used. The best, but the most expensive, is wood post-and-rail fencing. This should be painted with creosote to preserve it and to discourage horses from chewing the wood. Paint should not be used as it may contain lead which could be poisonous.

Otherwise, plain heavy gauge wire strung tightly from wooden posts is perfectly satisfactory. The lowest strand should not, however, be less than one foot from the ground in case an animal should catch a foot in the strand. Barbed wire, chicken mesh, old bedsteads and the like are not suitable fencing materials for horse paddocks.

Whatever type of fencing is used it is always a wise precaution to round off the corners of a field. Right angle corners can be a cause of serious accidents if horses start galloping about.

Salt blocks and/or mineral licks should be put out in the paddocks. Not only do they add to the horse's diet but their presence will often discourage the habit of chewing wood or the more annoying one of chewing the bark from trees (a practice which kills the trees eventually).

Foreign bodies, in the way of plastic containers, broken bottles, tins, pieces of old iron and so on, should be removed for obvious reasons. It is also necessary to check hedgerows for poisonous shrubs or trees. Yew is the worst offender, but deadly nightshade, briony, ivies and ragwort are also a danger.

Horses at grass need to be checked regularly for injury and to see that they are not ailing. The water, too, must be looked at and the fences inspected.

Horses in light work when at grass can be kept with their shoes on, but this is not necessary for a horse that is turned out and is not going to work at all. However, the feet will still need to be trimmed and rasped down regularly.

When hay is fed it is best given in haynets tied up as high as possible to the paddock rail. This is less wasteful than the practice of putting hay on the ground where it can be trodden under foot.

Stabling

Horses are kept in stables because they can be more easily managed for work, with less inconvenience to the owner. A stabled horse is more easily made fit for hard work. It is easier to keep clean and is always to hand when wanted. For all that, a stabled horse represents many hours of hard work each day.

The first essential when this method of horse-keeping is practised is, of course, the stable itself. It must meet three requirements. It must be well ventilated, but without draughts, well insulated and have an effective system of drainage.

The best type of accommodation is a loose-box, measuring ideally about 14 ft (4·3 m) × 12 ft (3·7 m). To ensure that it remains airy the ideal height to the eaves would be about 12 ft (3·7 m). Wide doorways, not less than 4 ft (1·2 m), which open outwards, are necessary if a horse is not to bang his hips going in and out. The height of the lower door should be 4 ft 6 in (1·4 m) which is high enough to discourage a horse from jumping out but not so high that he cannot see over.

Two bolts are necessary on the bottom half of the door: one on the top and one of the kickover type at the bottom in case the horse learns how to undo the top bolt.

Boxes are best sited facing south and out of headwinds. They should also be placed so that a horse can see what is going on. Hens, dogs and people walking about all help to keep a horse interested.

Stalls are another form of stabling, but not so satisfactory. As the horse is tied by the head, it has to spend most of the day staring at a blank wall.

Electric light switches should be placed outside boxes where horses cannot interfere with them. Windows should be placed next to the doorway, and should open inwards from a bottom hinge so that air enters in an upward direction and not directly on the horse. Drains, for obvious reasons, are best placed outside rather than inside the box.

The equipment necessary inside the

One of a horse's greatest pleasures is to have the freedom to graze and idle away the day in pastures of sweet grasses and herbs. Horses relax when out at grass and the freedom, as well as the nutritious spring growths, is wonderful for youngsters. In winter, however, horses kept out need a shelter and rations of hay and concentrate food.

Grooming equipment

Horses are groomed for the sake of appearance and to keep the skin clean and healthy. A stabled horse needs grooming every day. Horses and ponies kept out at grass in the winter should not be groomed because brushing would remove the protective natural grease from their coats. Water brushes are used on manes and tails, dandy brushes on legs.

dandy brush

body brush

curry comb

mane comb

sponge

water brush

Above: Young foals, like young children, learn by watching, touching and copying. This young foal that will still be getting his mother's milk, is now learning to eat grass by copying his dam. *Below:* A mare and foal indulge in a little mutual nibbling, which is most probably a sign of affection. Young foals respond to being scratched on the shoulders, back and rump.

The curry comb is used to clean the brush. It is not used on the horse's body unless it is of the rubber sort.

hoof oil and brush

hay wisp

hoof pick

stable rubber

rubber curry comb

box is a manger, a tie ring for attaching the horse, and also a haynet, and either an automatic drinking bowl or a heavy bucket that cannot easily be tipped over. Mangers are best positioned in a corner holder at breast height.

Chief requirements

Given a suitable box the requirements of the stabled horse are that he should be supplied with a bed, fed, groomed and exercised. The first contributes to his comfort and wellbeing, the other three combine to condition him for the work for which he is intended.

The best bedding is deep wheat straw. A deep bed encourages the horse to lie down. A thin bed can cause injuries from contact with the floor although in any case the horse may be reluctant to lie down on it.

Sawdust can be used for bedding but requires more management. Wood shavings are also used and are more satisfactory but are not absorbent like straw. Peat moss can also be used and recently a bedding material made from paper strips has been marketed.

Droppings should be removed from the box at regular intervals during the day. First thing in the mornings the bed is mucked out, i.e. all the wet and soiled straw is removed and the remainder banked round the edges of the box. The bed is relaid after exercise and then prepared for the night later in the day.

Feeding

Feeding is governed by three basic rules: 1. Feed little and often, 2. Do not work immediately after the horse has eaten, and 3. Always ensure that plenty of clean water is available.

Natural food for a horse is grass. Although stabled horses are not fed grass, the aim is to feed as nearly as possible to the natural way. This avoids straining the natural system of digestion. The horse has a very small stomach in relation to his size. His digestive system is designed to cope with an almost constant intake of food which is possible when a horse is out in a field grazing at will. The horse's very large bowel slowly digests the food that is taken in. In fact when the stomach is two-thirds full, food is passed to the bowels at the same rate as it enters the mouth.

Stabled horses are fed 'concentrates', or small amounts of high-protein food. Artificial foods distend the small

Two friends sharing a particularly tasty morsel. Horses appreciate a variety of grasses in their grazing areas and seem to be fond of a few sharp-tasting herbs, like chicory and plantain.

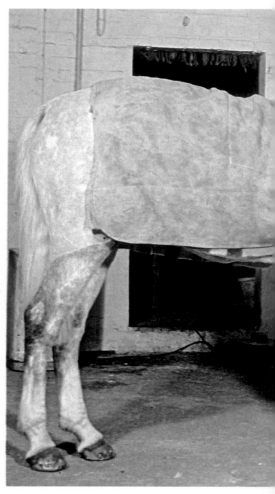

stomach, and large quantities of concentrate upset the digestive process and can result in attacks of colic (i.e. acute stomach-ache). No more than 3–4 lb (1·4–1·8 kg) of concentrates should, therefore, be given at any one feed. Hay, which acts as a digestive aid, can be given in larger quantities because it is always eaten slowly.

Horses are not worked following a meal because when the stomach is full and distended it presses upon the diaphragm which separates the stomach from the lungs. Any fast work which makes the lungs expand will not only make breathing difficult but will interfere with the digestive process and could cause severe colic.

Water is a life essential and plays an important part in digesting food. It must be freely available at all times.

Food for horses must contain the essential constituents of a balanced diet i.e. protein, fats, starches and sugar, water, fibrous roughage, salts and vitamins. Suitable foods can be divided into three groups: bulk foods, energy foods and auxiliaries.

Bulk foods consist principally of hay, chaff (a mixture of chopped hay and oat straw mixed with concentrates to prevent the horse bolting his food), specially made horse 'nuts' (although these also provide energy in different degrees), bran and green food (carrots, apples, turnips etc.). Grass also provides bulk.

Energy foods are represented by oats, barley, maize, beans and peas, and to a certain extent horse nuts.

Auxiliaries are foods like bran, cod-liver oil, linseed, feed-additives of various kinds, carrots, roots etc.

How much food and in what balance depends on the individual horse, its condition, and how much and what kind of work it is required to do.

As a good general guide, however, a horse of 15 hh requires a total daily food intake of 26 lb (11·5 kg). For larger and smaller horses add or subtract 2 lb (1 kg) for every 2 in (5 cm) of height (a hand, measures 4 in, 102 mm).

A horse in moderate work which is exercised each day and hunted one day a week needs an equal proportion of concentrates to bulk. For example, a 15 hh horse would eat 13 lb (5·9 kg) hay, the bulk of which would be given last thing at night, and 13 lb (5·9 kg) concentrates given in three or possibly four feeds. For a horse in very light work the proportion could be two-thirds bulk to one third concentrates. For a horse in very hard, fast work the proportions might be reversed, although it would never be possible to decrease the bulk food intake below this level.

Grooming and exercise

Grooming and exercise are the remaining elements in the conditioning and well-being of the stabled horse. Both take place each day and both are made easier in the winter months if the coat is removed by clipping. If the horse is clipped it is easier to keep it clean. The animal can also be worked harder and at faster speeds without losing body condition through excessive sweating. The most usual type of clip is called the 'hunter' clip. In this case a saddle patch of hair is left on the back and the hair is only lightly trimmed on the legs. A 'full' clip is when all the coat is removed. There are then variations on the 'trace' clip, which was originally intended for harness horses. In this type of clip the hair is removed from the underside of the neck, the flanks and belly, leaving a protective coat over the back and on the legs. It is frequently used on horses living out in New Zealand rugs or even on those spending much of the day in the paddock.

However, the removal of the natural coat means that the horse must be kept warm when it is not working or being exercised. Stabled horses are usually given rugs. Often an under-blanket and a top rug are used which are kept in place either by a roller round the body or a surcingle, or strap, attached to the rug. Wool leg bandages, put on below the knee or hock and carried down so as to cover the fetlock joints, are also part of the stabled horse's equipment. So, too, is the tail bandage, which helps to lay the tail neatly. In summer stabled

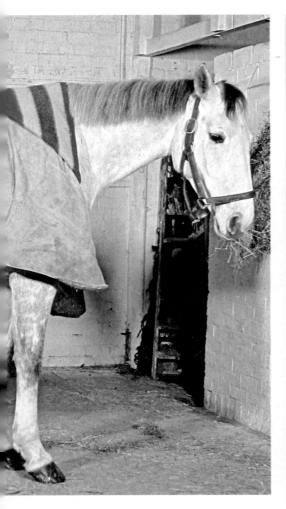

Three aspects concerned with the care of stabled horses are illustrated in these pictures. *Left:* The visit of the farrier. Feet need attention every five to six weeks and new shoes fitted if necessary. In any case it is necessary for the feet to be regularly trimmed. *Above:* A clipped horse, whose thick winter coat has been replaced by an underblanket and top rug so that it will be kept warm. *Right:* A horse being clipped at the end of the autumn. Horses are clipped so that they can be worked without undue sweating and so that they can be kept clean more easily.

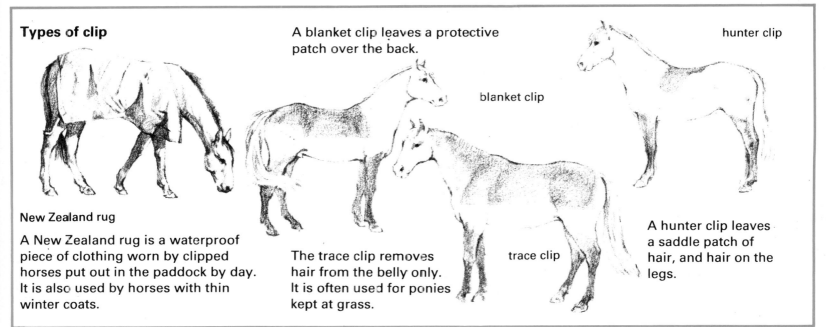

Types of clip

A blanket clip leaves a protective patch over the back.

hunter clip

blanket clip

trace clip

New Zealand rug

A New Zealand rug is a waterproof piece of clothing worn by clipped horses put out in the paddock by day. It is also used by horses with thin winter coats.

The trace clip removes hair from the belly only. It is often used for ponies kept at grass.

A hunter clip leaves a saddle patch of hair, and hair on the legs.

horses are usually fitted with cotton sheets to keep the coat clean.

Grooming includes the brushing out of mane and tail, the cleaning out of feet, the wiping of nose and dock and the thorough cleaning of the body by energetic brushing. It is vital to keep the horse in good health and begins early in the day when the horse is 'quartered' before going out to exercise. 'Quartering' is the equivalent of a 'lick and promise'. It is so-called because the rug is thrown back while the forehand is brushed and then rolled forward to allow the groom to clean the hindquarters. A thorough grooming (taking up to an hour or more) is given when the horse returns from daily exercise.

Exercise must be given every day for not less than one and a half hours. If this is not possible because of injury or some other cause, then the intake of energy food must be reduced at once. The last principle of feeding is that *the input of energy foods must be equalled by a corresponding energy output.*

Right: Companionship. This young foal, given the freedom of the yard, has quickly made friends with the dog.
Below: A chore in any stable is tack-cleaning. It is, however, very necessary for tack to be cleaned every day after use if it is to remain soft, supple and serviceable. It must also be carefully checked for signs of wear.

need to be checked regularly in case the rug should have slipped out of position. A well made New Zealand rug should always remain in place but not all are fitted with correctly positioned leg straps.

Unlike other rugs a New Zealand is made of waterproof material, and is only half-lined with blanketing. A fully lined rug would get the lower parts wet and muddy when the horse rolled.

Finally, horseowners should be able to diagnose and treat simple wounds and minor ailments. They need to keep and maintain a first-aid box containing scissors, bandages, colic drinks, healing powders, ointments, Vaseline etc.

Left: Auctions of saddlery and harness take place at many markets and horse sales and it is sometimes possible to pick up a bargain. Sometimes, however, such sales are outlets for poor quality goods. *Below:* This grey horse looks interested, content and happy—which is just what is wanted!

Shoeing and tack

The feet of the horse must be kept clean, and seen to regularly by the blacksmith. Metal shoes are necessary to protect the feet of a working horse. The horn of the horse's foot grows at the rate of between a quarter to three-eighths of an inch (6·3–9·5 mm) each month and therefore needs attention every four or five weeks. Horses doing a lot of work on the roads will usually need new shoes at this time. Some will simply require the feet to be trimmed and the existing shoes replaced.

When the horse has been fed and watered (four times a day), groomed and exercised and the box mucked out, what time is left to the groom is used to keep the horse's saddlery, or tack, clean, soft and supple. Usual items include a headcollar, bridle, saddle, girth, leathers and irons and probably boots and exercising bandages too!

The combined system

The work of looking after a horse can be reduced by keeping it on the 'combined system'. As its name suggests, this combines elements from the systems of keeping the horse out at grass, and keeping it stabled. In practice, this method, with individual variations in the time spent at grass, is probably the one most widely used in temperate climates. The horse is put out in his paddock in a New Zealand rug for several hours a day. In this way he can exercise himself, if only to a certain extent, and the stable is kept clean. Of course, he still needs feeding and grooming, and New Zealand rugs need maintenance if they are to remain satisfactory. Horses wearing them

Chapter nine
Working with Horses

Despite long hours, working with horses is very rewarding. There are lots of opportunities if you are prepared to work hard — as an instructor, perhaps, or even in the old skills of farriery or saddlery.

There are a variety of careers connected with horses open to young people. But at the outset it is only fair to say that working with horses is not for clock-watchers, the would-be makers of quick money or for the work-shy. Nor, really, is it for those who love horses but think of them in terms of riding alone. For every hour actually spent on a horse's back there are half a dozen to be spent at the sheer hard work of looking after it. Horses are, indeed, a vocation to those that work with them and a daunting degree of dedication to the job is needed. That said, although financial rewards are never very high, horses give a great degree of job satisfaction and for many they become the core of a way of life.

Teaching others to ride
For those with a feeling for teaching, there are jobs as instructors in riding schools. In most countries some sort of qualification is needed for this work, although there is nothing to stop anyone from teaching riding so long as there are sufficient customers prepared to pay for tuition. Most schools, however, ask for qualifications which are usually awarded by a national governing body. Colleges of education, and riding schools organize a variety of courses which lead to a qualifying examination. Government grants are sometimes available for these courses and most young people get started by being accepted at one or other of the major schools as a 'working pupil'. They pay for board and lodging but

Left: A happy partnership between a young rider and her sensible sort of pony. A pony of this kind, who is good-natured and not too highly-strung, is the most suitable for the average child. *Right:* This young lady is taking her responsibilities seriously but she should be *brushing* the tail out, not using a comb which will only break and pull out the hairs.

receive instruction in return for work, which usually means a six a.m. start and not much time off. Candidates are usually expected to remain at the school for a period of at least one year. In all cases it is advisable for the candidate to be a reasonably proficient rider before starting the course.

Not everyone, of course, wants to teach others to ride and, indeed, there are not that many who are able. There are, however, careers as stable managers. There are usually special courses and exams specially designed to qualify people for this very important position.

Working as a groom
For those who do not, perhaps, aspire as high as this there are openings for grooms in riding schools, livery yards, yards specializing in the production of show horses, jumpers or eventers, as well as in privately owned stables. Again, many countries run courses and

Regular grooming of the horse's body, the brushing out of mane and tail and the cleaning out of the feet are part of the daily routine of good horse-keeping.

examinations for people wishing to take up these kinds of job.

Well qualified and highly competent grooms can not only command good salaries but they can also, to a certain extent, choose their jobs throughout the world. A good groom in a show jumping stable, for instance, has an enormously interesting job and is involved in travelling extensively with his or her horses. As well as being good riders and very proficient horse masters, such grooms must be able to drive horse-boxes and generally be very self-reliant characters. Much of the success of the enterprise depends upon the good groom. He must be superlatively good at keeping horses fit and in good order, and in keeping their equipment clean and serviceable. He

Above: Working on a stud farm can be very rewarding. Here is a really good type of young foal, alert and full of life. It has a neat head, well set on the neck, a compact body and very good limbs with big, strong joints. *Left:* Another good sort of horse. Although not beautiful this whipper-in's horse, which is well enough made, will probably carry him very well all day. This is important for a hunt horse which must take tough country in its stride.

must also be a support and helpmate to the rider. The same, of course, applies to grooms in the competitive sports of dressage, eventing and even driving, where a very specialized knowledge is needed.

There are also interesting jobs for grooms in hunt stables. Keeping a stable of hunt horses going throughout a hunting season is a very highly skilled job and a real challenge, for hunt horses have to work hard in difficult conditions. These jobs, of course, may not continue through the summer months when the hunt horses will be put out to grass. Many grooms in hunt stables go to work with polo ponies in the summer.

There are limited opportunities for employment in hunt service proper, i.e. as a huntsman or whipper-in, and in this field experience and a devotion to the sport are essential.

Working on a stud farm

There are deeply satisfying careers to be made in stud work for those who enjoy looking after animals but are not very bothered about riding horses. The ability to ride, however, is always an advantage, particularly if you are light and able to back young horses i.e. break them in for riding under saddle.

The stud farm is at the base of all horse activity and there are usually examinations for stud workers. In fact, a number of colleges run courses on horse-management with stud farm careers as the principal objective.

The variety of opportunity open to suitably experienced stud hands is very large. It ranges from work on smaller studs producing ponies to the palatial studs at Newmarket, England, or at Lexington, Kentucky. At such studs, Thoroughbred racehorses are bred and the stock may be valued at millions of pounds or dollars.

Thoroughbreds, of course, mean racing and there are careers at both steeplechase and flat racing stables for boys and girls. In both worlds the starting point is at the bottom of the ladder. A 'lad' in a racing yard 'does' two or more racehorses, looking after them and riding them at exercise. From there on it is a matter of talent and, for those that show promise, there are a number of races in which their boss, the trainer, can enter them. Success depends on talent and, to a certain extent, on luck. But at the top of either tree, whether 'chasing or flat racing, the rewards are high. Successful jockeys, many of whom go into training when they hang up their boots, are often wealthy men. It must, however, be admitted that of the two, flat racing is the less hazardous and the more lucrative.

Veterinary surgeons and nurses

The veterinary profession also offers scope for employment for those interested in horses. After qualifying at university, veterinary surgeons can specialize in horse practice. There are also openings as veterinary assistants or nurses, who do not require a university degree. Nurses require certain qualifications, however, and in Britain, for instance, the Royal College of Veterinary Surgeons supervise the training and registration of Registered Animal Nursing Auxiliaries, who are known by the initials RANA. It takes two years to train and two qualifying examinations have to be passed. Candidates can, however, be trained while working with a veterinary surgeon and during that period they receive a salary. Otherwise courses are run at the various veterinary colleges.

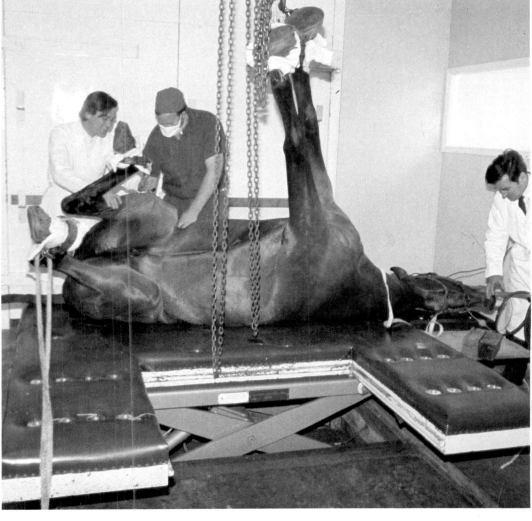

Above: Hopefully, racehorses like these, out for the early morning exercise, will not need the attention of the veterinary surgeon. But accidents do happen and horses, like humans, can suffer from disease and sickness. *Below:* It is, therefore, comforting to know how expert is the veterinary attention available today and how up-to-date is the equipment which can be used.

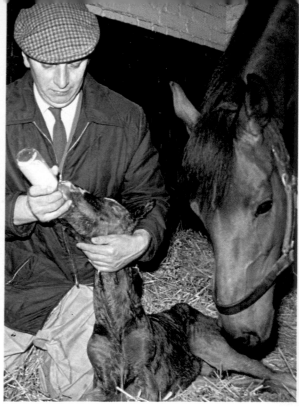

Veterinary science at work. *Above:* An 'intensive care unit' is set up to nurse an ailing foal. *Above right:* A very young foal, unable to feed normally, is being bottle-fed. *Below:* The patient has been anaesthetized on the operating table and the veterinary surgeon is making an examination of the mouth. In recent years, often due to the work done at establishments like Newmarket's Equine Research Station, veterinary science has made remarkable progress in the diagnosis and treatment of horse ailments. Working in such an establishment is a rewarding job.

There is usually a big demand for veterinary nurses who undertake very responsible work, assisting at operations and with animals retained for post-operative care.

Farriery

The profession of farriery is sometimes overlooked when careers connected with horses are being considered. But it is fundamental to the use and welfare of horses. For a young man with the right aptitudes, however, (and this seems to be a career more suited to men than women) farriery offers a secure and well paid future. Farriers are not just 'bangers-on of horse shoes'. They are specialists in the needs of horse's hooves and lower limbs, and are often consulted by veterinary surgeons.

In many countries entry into this profession is by an apprenticeship, served with a Master Farrier, of not less than four years. Examinations have to be passed during this time. Finally, an apprentice can set up in business as a qualified farrier and take on apprentices of his own if he so wishes.

For those not wishing to run their own businesses most racing stables, and many large studs and showing stables employ full-time farriers.

Saddlery

The craft of saddlery is one that is certainly open to young people of either sex. Again, opportunities are plentiful and there are good livings to be made. As with farriery, entrance is probably best made by becoming an apprentice to a Master Saddler but there are also colleges in many countries which encourage rural crafts and which run comprehensive courses in the various aspects of saddlery. The craft of saddlery is complex and highly skilled. The trade

is divided into harness makers, who produce the equipment for driving horses; saddle makers; bridle makers, as well as those who make leather goods of all kinds. The other great advantage of the saddlery business is that there are usually opportunities for those who want to set up on their own.

In most countries there are numerous retail saddlers' shops. These are usually staffed by informed assistants who can give constructive advice to their customers.

Selling, in fact, has quite a lot to offer. Apart from saddlers' shops there are hundreds of firms manufacturing horse requisites, medicines and foods which employ teams of sales representatives as well as fairly large office and works staffs. The connection with the horse may at first seem to be tenuous but it is there nonetheless, and these industries are an essential part of the horse world.

Riding in the forces

The services and the police forces also offer opportunities for working with horses. Most countries maintain mounted military detachments for ceremonial occasions. The mounted branches of police forces have a particular and very important role to play. Mounted police are employed to patrol city streets and to assist in controlling crowds at events such as football matches, protest marches and so on. One policeman mounted on a horse, in situations where crowd control is necessary, is reckoned to be equal to ten or more officers on foot.

Mounted police are regarded as the elite of the force and entry into this branch can be applied for only after a period of service in one of the force's more usual branches. In general, mounted police are employed as part of

Stages in shoeing

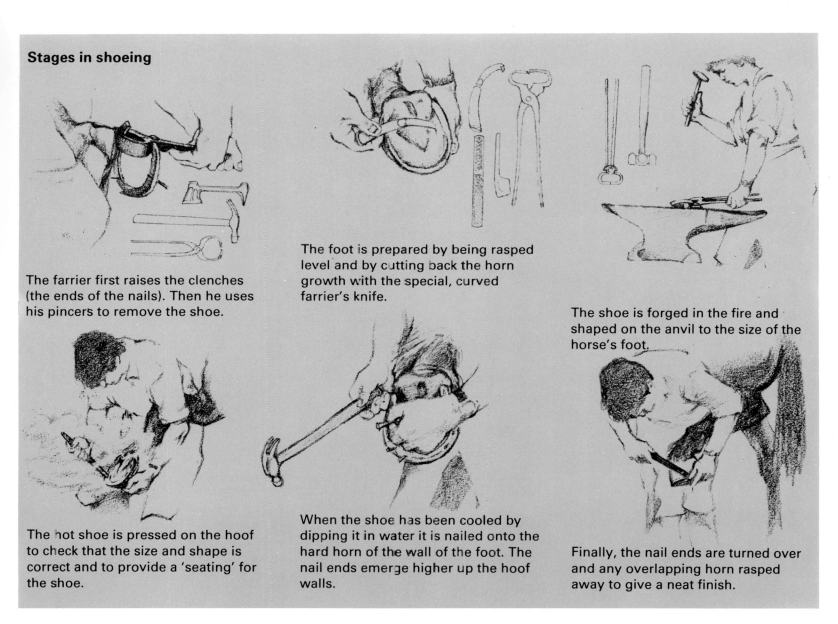

The farrier first raises the clenches (the ends of the nails). Then he uses his pincers to remove the shoe.

The foot is prepared by being rasped level and by cutting back the horn growth with the special, curved farrier's knife.

The shoe is forged in the fire and shaped on the anvil to the size of the horse's foot.

The hot shoe is pressed on the hoof to check that the size and shape is correct and to provide a 'seating' for the shoe.

When the shoe has been cooled by dipping it in water it is nailed onto the hard horn of the wall of the foot. The nail ends emerge higher up the hoof walls.

Finally, the nail ends are turned over and any overlapping horn rasped away to give a neat finish.

the force operative in larger city areas. It is important to realize that military mounted detachments are first and foremost soldiers and are required to have a soldier's skills as well as those of a horseman.

Conditions in both army and police units nowadays are very attractive. Both offer secure careers with excellent prospects of promotion and a wide variety of opportunities for horsemanship.

As with any career, hard work and some talent are necessary attributes in those who intend to be successful with horses. On the other hand, a career with horses can be a fascinating one. If you are good enough, there are always plenty of opportunities to set up as your own master.

If you you join the army or the police force in order to work with horses you may find yourself riding some very fine horses. Although the Lipizzaner is commonly associated with the Spanish School of Vienna, the horses are bred elsewhere in Europe too, notably Yugoslavia, Czechoslovakia and Hungary. These stallions are being trained for military work in Yugoslavia.

Index

Page numbers in italics refer to illustrations.

Acknowledgements

The publishers would like to thank the following individuals and organizations for their kind permission to reproduce the pictures in this book:
AFA 7; All-Sport (Steve Powell) 43; Animal Photography 7, 63, 68–69 (Sally-Anne Thompson) 13, 19, 20, 25, 28, 30, 33, 47, 54, 74; Ardea (I R Beames) 9 (John Gooders) 65 (Sue Gooders) 65; Bavaria-Verlag 22; John Carnemolia 2–3, 51; Bruce Coleman (Jane Burton) 8 (R Meek) 59 (Hans Reinhard) 21, 74 (J van Wormer) 25; Colour Library International 15, 22, 23; Colorsport 39; Anne Cumbers 34, 69; Arthur Dailey, Wyoming 24; Daily Telegraph Colour Library 57, 60, 75; F Davidson 45; Expression 32; James Fain, Utah 28, 29; Graham Finlayson 35, 38, 43, 48; Fox Photos 61; Globe (J R Hamilton) 29; Robert Harding 18; Michael Holford 26–27; Keystone 60; Paolo Koch 31; E D Lacey 42, 44, 46, 47, 54; Claire Leimbach 68; John Meads 41; Jane Miller 12; John Moss 36, 37, 70, 72; Pictor 16–17, 56; Picturepoint 31; Popperfoto 67; Rapho Picture Agency 10–11; Realites (M Desjardines) 4–5; Mike Roberts 49; Peter Roberts 50, 53, 55; Peter D Rossdale 75, 76; W W Rouch & Co. 61; Iantha Ruthven 1; Spanish Riding School of Vienna 14; Spectrum 36, 64, 71, 73; Tony Stone 6 (Sue Streeter) 52; Syndication International 40; Elizabeth Weiland 18, 58, 59, 76; Zefa (B Benjamin) 77 (Hans Reinhard) 66 (M Thonig) 71.